SD 392 .G37 1995
Garfitt, J. E. 1914-
Natural management of woods

Natural Management of Woods:
Continuous Cover Forestry

FORESTRY SERIES

Series Editor: **Esmond H. M. Harris,** BSc., Dip.For., FICFor., CBiol., MIBiol.

1. COMPUTERS IN FORESTRY: Use of Spreadsheets
   Roy Lorrain-Smith

2. Natural Management of Woods: Continuous Cover Forestry*
   J. E. Garfitt

* Front cover illustration:
Group regeneration in beech and mixed conifers in southern France

Group Selection in a Gloucestershire beechwood

Group Selection in beech and spruce in the Belgian Ardennes

Natural Management of Woods: Continuous Cover Forestry

J. E. Garfitt
MA(Oxon)

RESEARCH STUDIES PRESS LTD.
Taunton, Somerset, England

JOHN WILEY & SONS INC.
New York · Chichester · Toronto · Brisbane · Singapore

RESEARCH STUDIES PRESS LTD.
24 Belvedere Road, Taunton, Somerset, England TA1 1HD

Copyright © 1995 by Research Studies Press Ltd.

All rights reserved.

No part of this book may be reproduced by any means,
nor transmitted, nor translated into a machine language
without the written permission of the publisher.

The right of John Edward Garfitt to be identified as the author
of this work has been asserted by him in accordance with
the Copyright, Designs and Patents Act, 1988.

Marketing and Distribution:

Australia and New Zealand:
Jacaranda Wiley Ltd.
GPO Box 859, Brisbane, Queensland 4001, Australia

Canada:
JOHN WILEY & SONS CANADA LIMITED
22 Worcester Road, Rexdale, Ontario, Canada

Europe, Africa, Middle East and Japan:
JOHN WILEY & SONS LIMITED
Baffins Lane, Chichester, West Sussex, England

North and South America:
JOHN WILEY & SONS INC.
605 Third Avenue, New York, NY 10158, USA

South East Asia:
JOHN WILEY & SONS (SEA) PTE LTD.
37 Jalan Pemimpin 05-04
Block B Union Industrial Building, Singapore 2057

Library of Congress Cataloging-in-Publication Data

Garfitt, J. E. (John Edward), 1914–
    Natural management of woods : continuous cover forestry / J.E.
  Garfitt.
        p.   cm. — (Forestry series ; 2)
    Includes index.
    ISBN 0-86380-171-4 (Research Studies Press Ltd.). — ISBN
  0-471-95569-8 (John Wiley & Sons Inc.)
    1. Silvicultural systems. 2. Forest management. 3. Forest
  reproduction. 4. Silvicultural systems—Great Britain. 5. Forest
  management—Great Britain. 6. Forest reproduction—Great Britain.
  I. Title. II. Series.
  SD392.G37   1995
  634.9′5—dc20   94-41783
                                                              CIP

British Library Cataloguing in Publication Data

A catalogue record for this book
is available from the British Library.

ISBN 0 86380 171 4 (Research Studies Press Ltd.)
ISBN 0 471 95569 8 (John Wiley & Sons Inc.)

Typeset by Abracadabra!, Milton Keynes, England
Printed in Great Britain by SRP Ltd., Exeter

Acknowledgements

Some chapters of this book contain material adapted from articles I have written over a long period of years and published in the *Quarterly Journal of Forestry* and in *Forestry*, the journals respectively of the Royal Forestry Society of England, Wales and Northern Ireland and of the Society of Foresters of Great Britain, now the Institute of Chartered Foresters.

I am indebted to John Matthews, Emeritus Professor of Forestry in the University of Aberdeen, for his kindness in agreeing to write the Preface to this book and also for permission to reproduce silvicultural diagrams from his *Silvicultural Systems*, published by the Oxford University Press 1989.

J.E. Garfitt
December 1994

Contents

Preface	Professor J.D. Matthews CBE, FICFOR.	xi
Chapter 1	Woods and forests for all	1
Chapter 2	Natural regeneration	7
Chapter 3	Assisted natural regeneration	17
Chapter 4	Natural regeneration systems in even-aged woods	23
Chapter 5	Natural regeneration systems in irregular woods: coppice-with-standards	29
Chapter 6	Natural regeneration systems in irregular woods: the selection system	37
Chapter 7	Natural regeneration systems in irregular woods: the group selection system	43
Chapter 8	Conversion to group selection of even-aged woods	47
Chapter 9	Conversion to group selection of unmanaged woodland and scrub	53
Chapter 10	Control of the felling in irregular woods	61
Chapter 11	Avoiding clear-felling in ornamental plantings	65

Chapter 12	Re-stocking by natural means	73
Chapter 13	Planting: some basic considerations	79
Chapter 14	Planting: systems	85
Chapter 15	Planting: techniques	93
Chapter 16	Weeding	99
Chapter 17	Cleaning, brashing, and de-wolfing	103
Chapter 18	Pruning	107
Chapter 19	Thinning: basic considerations	111
Chapter 20	Thinning: techniques	117
Chapter 21	Felling	125
Chapter 22	Extraction	129
Chapter 23	Big trees and compound interest	137
Index		141

Preface

Since the early 1950s Mr J.E. Garfitt has become well-known as one of an adventurous and talented group of foresters who have specialized in the management of woodlands in the lowlands of Britain that are mixed in species and uneven-aged or irregular in structure. In particular he has devised and adapted systems of silviculture suitable for restoring broadleaved woodlands that had been made unproductive by past exploitation fellings or through neglect, or are in danger of being lost because of old age.

Mr Garfitt has recorded the results of his long and varied experience clearly and convincingly. The book is important because it provides ideas and methods that have been thoroughly tested in practice for raising tree-crops that produce timber of good quality, in conditions that maintain and enhance amenity, improve public access to woodlands where this is required, conserve wild plants, animals and birds, and cater for field sports. All this is done with close attention to costs and improving estate finances by the production and sale of timber and other forest produce, by improving facilities for field sports and by adding to the attractions of those estates that actively cater for the public.

The potential value of 'natural management' through 'continuous cover forestry' to the development of woodlands on many private estates is becoming recognized. A very important contributory factor is that woods already exist and are often due or overdue for replacement. Using the methods described by Mr Garfitt the growing stock of trees can be brought to the condition needed for sustained yield. Large clear-fellings are avoided in favour of small clearings, and natural regeneration is used whenever possible. Because the area of woodlands on many private estates is relatively small, the emphasis in silviculture and management is on improving the quality of the growing stock so that as much high-quality timber as possible is produced.

In Chapter 1, 'Woods and Forests for All', the ideas summarized above are expanded and some special features of broad-leaved woodlands in the lowlands are explained. Chapters 2 and 3 contain discussions of the values of natural regeneration and the difficulties encountered by forest managers in using natural seedlings to re-stock their woods. There is much good practical advice here, especially about methods of ground preparation to make a good seed-bed, transplanting seedlings from overstocked to understocked areas and enrichment of existing regeneration with plants of good genetic quality.

The next four chapters describe silvicultural systems used in even-aged, or regular, and in uneven-aged, or irregular, woodlands. The account of the Coppice-with-Standards system in Chapter 5 is particularly useful because it emphasizes the advantages (early returns from the coppice, good cover for game, high conservation value and attractive appearance) and then suggests ways of appraising the system where the provision of continuous tree cover is being sought. Alternative species to hazel for the coppice underwood are suggested and the need to think about the desired proportions of timber, pulpwood and fuelwood is stressed. This old and honourable system is often favoured by conservationists; Mr Garfitt suggests that they should consult an experienced forester to get the best results from its use.

In Chapter 7 the development of the Group Selection System in Britain is outlined. In Chapters 8 and 9 the application of this system to the conversion of even-aged woods and unmanaged woodland and scrub to 'continuous cover forestry' is described in detail. In Chapter 10 methods of controlling fellings in irregular woodlands are discussed; a proposal is made for yield control by area.

In my opinion, the Group Selection System with its emphasis on the clearance and re-stocking of small areas is well-suited to the conditions existing in many woods and forests in lowland Britain; the system can also be used in parts of the uplands regularly visited by the public. The size of groups can be varied to meet the silvicultural needs of species, exploit the occurrence of natural regeneration, and retain older trees for as long as their increment is sustained. Growing trees in groups maintains competition between them and satisfies an essential element of their ecology. The forest manager can also take advantage of relations between species — described in this book as nursing, and 'edge-effects' (in Chapter 13). Finally, there is the amenity created by the varying appearance of the groups differing in species and age, and also by a long-term constancy of view over the whole woodland area.

Chapter 11 on avoiding clear-felling in ornamental plantations is particularly valuable for those who wish to restore the splendid work of past landscape architects, particularly Lancelot 'Capability' Brown and Humphrey Repton. The trees planted singly during the 18th century, in groves, avenues, screens, and shelterbelts, are now often in need of replacement; several possible solutions are described and their usefulness analyzed. The conclusion reached is that the principal aim when dealing with old woods or old park plantings should be to determine as clearly as possible the original intentions of the planters and to re-create these so as to achieve the same or closely similar effects.

Re-stocking by natural means (Chapter 12) is chiefly an account of the silviculture of species that produce suckers readily. One such species is wild cherry or gean and I know from past experience of this useful species in eastern Scotland that thriving and productive stands can originate from suckers.

Chapters 13 to 22 form a complete silvicultural and managerial guide, beginning with planting (Chapters 13, 14, and 15), cleaning, brashing and de-wolfing (Chapter 17), pruning (Chapter 18), thinning (Chapters 19 and 20), felling (Chapter 21) and extraction of the produce (Chapter 22). These pages distil a wealth of practical knowledge about simple yet effective methods of treating woods from the earliest stages to the final harvesting of mature trees. Most modern techniques are examined and carefully appraised. I missed reference to mobile wood-chippers — which have been effectively used when cleaning and thinning late-thicket stage broad-leaved crops — but would accept that they need further appraisal in this role. The theme throughout these chapters is attention to the care of suitable individual trees or groups of trees that show promise of producing timber of high quality. This work begins with selection of planting stock of good inherent quality and continues until stems free from faults emerge for the market. The same attention to detail applies to improving access for field sports and constructing roads for harvesting timber.

The final chapter (23) deals with a subject that has tended to dominate the planting phase of British forestry, namely that of economic appraisals based on discounted costs of planting set against discounted values of sales of forest produce. The method was devised in Germany during the middle of the 19th century to guide investors who wished to plant Norway spruce on abandoned farmland. It was very useful for this purpose and has also proved useful in financing the afforestation of the uplands in Britain. However, when the second generation of forests arrives, as is the case on many private estates in the lowlands, the existing crop must be replaced because the forest law says so. In these circumstances replanting becomes a charge against the previous crop and the state offers grants to help defray the costs of regeneration. Thus I find myself in close agreement with Mr Garfitt's statement that because felling and regeneration are operations basic to forestry new replacement crops should not normally carry the burden of interest charges. Of course, it remains important that the whole forestry enterprise must pay its way from year to year.

It remains for me to recommend this book to those who will certainly gain from reading it. First and foremost are owners of woodlands and their forestry advisers in the lowlands. Second, are those landowners and foresters who support continuous cover forestry in other situations, including the uplands; they are sure to benefit from Mr Garfitt's experience, ideas and methods. Third, are practical conservationists who wish to practise 'natural forestry', and seek expert guidance. Fourth, are students of forestry who need all the practical guidance they can get. Fifth, are those who need to understand the skills that a forester can bring to his profession; these include land use planners and members of other land-use professions. There will be more; let us hope there are many more who will wish to savour Ted Garfitt's wisdom!

John Matthews
4, Riverbank Close,
Heswall, Wirral
October 1994

CHAPTER 1

Woods and Forests for All

There is now so much interest in trees and woodland that the reason for their existence is apt to be forgotten. Without the trees the land would be bare; without the foresight of former owners in re-stocking their woods they would not exist today. In recent times only a small proportion of woods have been planted for their amenity value; the majority owe their existence to their value as timber producers, that is as generators of money.

In order therefore to see the picture as a whole it is necessary to accept the fact that the management of woods must ensure that there is a satisfactory return to the owner. How this is to be achieved while giving due weight to considerations of amenity, access, and conservation is examined in the following chapters. It will be seen that the adoption of one of the systems of woodland management covered by the term Continuous Cover Systems has much to offer as a solution. This principle postulates that the soil and the ecosystem are of prime importance and that interference with either should be kept to the minimum. As, however, woodlands do not exist primarily for the use of investigating scientists nor for the enjoyment of visitors, but have to pay their way, this principle has to be applied in a manner that permits the growing and harvesting of timber. The most satisfactory methods of doing this have proved to be what are known to foresters as the Selection and Group Selection Systems. In France they are known as *jardinage* and *jardinage par bouquets*; that is, gardening and gardening in clumps. These systems, which will be dealt with in some detail, result in woodland whose appearance never changes overall, although local change is continually taking place. Under these systems there is never any clear-felling.

There is a tendency these days to regard amenity as of concern only to the outside observer whereas it is of course of even more intense interest to the owner or occupier of a property. Happily the two points of view generally coincide. What is beautiful to the owner of an estate is almost without exception appreciated by the general public, particularly if there are suitable viewpoints or some degree of access.

It is widely accepted that the clear-felling of large areas of woodland is undesirable where such areas can be seen from public roads; and this is especially so on hill slopes. The clear-felling on private estates of old woodland is also deplored where such woods are an essential part of the original estate layout, designed by Repton, Brown, or other master landscapers. Any owner is sad to contemplate the destruction of a familiar pattern that cannot be reproduced within a period of perhaps a hundred years. Visitors to such an estate — and many are now open to the public at least to a limited extent — are apt to regard such felling as desecration.

With a disproportionally large urban population in Britain there is a constant demand for increased access to the countryside. Open moorland and woodland in particular are the subject of attention, and the vast plantations of the Forestry Commission only partly satisfy the need that people feel for something approximating to wilderness. The city-dweller, living in a confined area in close proximity to his fellow workers, requires space and a feeling of freedom.

This need has been met to an ever-increasing degree by the opening of large country estates anxious to remain solvent in a time of crippling taxation and falling farm incomes. The big country houses and their pleasure-grounds provide ideal surroundings for many, but there is still an unsatisfied demand for room to walk in traditional woodland. This has been recognized by successive governments, and grants to woodland owners to assist with the cost of re-stocking felled woods are made subject to agreement that access to the woods will be made available.

It is at this point that sport, in particular pheasant-shooting, produces complications. This is a traditional country sport enjoyed by the majority of land-owners. It has also in recent years acquired a special social significance. The majority of shoots today are operated on a syndicate basis, being let to a group of enthusiasts, the owner often retaining an interest. The ability to invite a friend or business acquaintance to shoot is highly valued, and shooting-rents reflect the demand for good, well-keepered shoots. But more or less intensive use of footpaths, or even casual trespass, over an estate are not compatible with the satisfactory production of pheasants and their 'showing' by the keepers on shooting days. The owner today gets more than the satisfaction of a few shooting days in the autumn and early winter; he receives a very useful rent. In fact the shooting-rent from an estate with well-placed woods and plantations may, under skilled management, provide greater returns than those obtainable from the woods themselves in the form of timber and other woodland products. Is he to forgo this, and the satisfaction of running his own estate as he wishes, by allowing access to his coverts?

This situation is not always fully appreciated by organizations demanding access to woodlands nor, it would seem, by government bodies concerned with woodland grants.

Conservation. The need to maintain optimum conditions for wildlife of all kinds is now well recognized. Its implementation in the woodland presents few basic problems. There is a need for all species of mammals, plants and insects native to an area to enjoy the conditions under which they can thrive within the limits of their own ecosystems. There must therefore be a proportion of the woodland area in which light can reach the ground in sufficient intensity to meet this requirement; there must be corridors of a suitable character along which the wild denizens of the wood can move in order to colonize fresh areas created by operations carried out in the woodland; and to this end in some cases suitable habitats must be provided artificially where woodland management would not ordinarily create them. The provision of the majority of these requirements can be achieved very simply by creating a full road and ride system at an early stage of the establishment of a new woodland area; or by the laying-out of a similar system in an existing woodland. The essential requirement is that the roads and rides should be of sufficient width to allow full light to reach the borders; that is, the part of the road or ride not actually compacted by the wheels of vehicles. While the trees are comparatively small, the road or ride need not be very wide, but as they grow the light reaching the borders will of course be reduced by their shading effect. This can be countered to a useful degree by removing all the trees bordering the road or ride in the first thinning. At this stage little shading-out of the ground flora will have taken place under these trees. Since their crowns will be of a spreading character on this side, where they have enjoyed full light, they will tend to be of larger girth, although probably more irregular in stem form, than those in the interior of the crop. They will, however, provide a useful component of the total volume of saleable material resulting from the first thinning.

Experience has shown that it does not pay to undertake intensive work on sites where trees will not otherwise grow successfully. Such preparatory work can be very expensive and if its cost is to be subject to compound interest the probability of its being justified is small. This fits in well with conservation considerations since such areas can, with little sacrifice, be left in a natural state. This applies particularly to small ponds and boggy areas of no great extent, where drainage would be difficult to mechanize. Again, a sufficiently large area should be left unplanted to ensure that adequate light will reach the site during the full life of the surrounding tree crop. The same general principles can be applied, without serious loss of productive land, to stream sides and rocky outcrops.

These general rules will meet the requirements of most forms of wildlife but there are some exceptions. It has always been a sound axiom of woodland management that woodland health is best ensured by the removal of potential disease-carrying material in the form of dead, dying, and decayed trees and fallen wood. This covers the felling of dead trees in which bark-beetles may breed and of diseased trees that may act as centres of infection by fungal diseases. But dead trees and old dying trees often provide unique nesting sites for a number of species of birds as well as breeding sites for non-injurious insects. They may also act as important hosts for lichens and other micro-flora and fauna. The biologist requires their retention in the woodland; to the manager they are an offence against his principles as well as his aesthetic taste. By all the rules of ordinary management they ought to be removed; no-one likes to display a vegetable garden containing dead cabbages and decaying rhubarb. A well-managed wood can be recognized at a glance; one containing dying trees and diseased trees is not acceptable to a conscientious manager. A way of meeting both these requirements is suggested. Biologists and conservationists require to have these trees retained; and this requirement puts a value on them. The trees concerned have no money-value to the manager but he suffers a loss in woodland hygiene if they are not felled. How much would the biologist or conservationist pay for them to be retained? How much would the manager be prepared to accept to tolerate their continued presence? It would seem that the former might be prepared to buy these trees as they stand, provided that they were not in any way interfered with. And the manager might be quite prepared to see them remain, provided that their presence did not interfere with the overall management and that they were paid for. It would be necessary for them to be clearly marked (say, in yellow paint) and identified as belonging to the purchasing body. This system would meet the requirements of both parties; the trees would remain standing and at the same time their presence could not be ascribed in any way to lack of good woodland management.

These considerations suggest a wider extension of the idea. Local conservation bodies are frequently concerned over the future of broadleaved woodland in their areas, and statutory controls rarely meet all their requirements. From their specialized point of view purchase is the only way to ensure that their aims can be achieved. Raising funds by public appeals has a limit and there are always more woods that these bodies would like to buy but for which they have no prospect of funds. Now, if such a body were prepared to buy a single dead tree, as suggested above, would it perhaps be prepared to buy a whole standing crop at its calculated value, discounted back? The owner would then receive the value of his crop, just as if he had managed it to the age at which it would normally been felled; he would therefore suffer no pecuniary loss. The conservation body would have complete control of the wood for the agreed period, for a sum far less than its current freehold value. In addition, both owner and purchaser would continue to enjoy the amenity value of the woodland.

This would present clear advantages to the owner. He would receive a very substantial return for the woodland; he would be freed from the cost of any maintenance for the remainder of the rotation; and he would resume occupation at the agreed date. The advantage to the conservation body would be that it would achieve control of the woodland more easily since the transfer would be to the owner's advantage; and more cheaply than by purchase since no price for the freehold would be involved and the cost of the standing crop would be discounted to its current value.

The adoption of such a means of selling and acquiring a crop of trees would provide a yardstick by which the amenity or conservation value of any wood could be assessed. This in turn would make possible the true valuation of what have hitherto been regarded as imponderables.

Mention has been made of the function of wide rides and roads as corridors allowing the migration of plant and insect species and the movement of animals from one part of the woodland to another. In areas where felling is in progress this contact is of particular importance. After any felling it is desirable that the newly exposed soil should be re-colonized as soon as possible by species native to the site and that the original ecosystem should be restored. The Group Selection System, which will be considered later, has particular advantages in this respect since open patches of limited extent are produced in reasonable proximity at comparatively short intervals. This provides opportunities for the re-establishment of ecosystems and of reserves from which newly-felled areas can be colonized. The advantages of this system can be appreciated when considered in contrast to clear-felling systems where large areas are felled at very long intervals.

This was well demonstrated where group-felling and replanting were undertaken in a large and decaying oakwood in north Lincolnshire. It was planned to replace the whole wood, of some 80 hectares, by progressive replanting, confining exposure to the newly-planted areas to the minimum. This was achieved by dividing the area into rectangular blocks of about one hectare, the longer sides running north and south. The order in which they were felled was so arranged that no planted area was ever exposed by new felling until it was sheltered on all sides, either by the old standing wood or by a planted crop at least five metres in height. These young plantations, which had not reached the stage of close canopy, still carried the old ground flora, which allowed for cross-colonization. Visiting officers of the local conservation trust confessed themselves much impressed by the opportunities the system provided for the re-establishment of ancient ecosystems over large areas due for clearing and replanting.

CHAPTER 2
Natural Regeneration

Almost all gardeners will be familiar with the problem of ash and sycamore seedlings, and probably those of yew as well, which have to be weeded out of their borders. They will require no convincing of the aggressive character of the colonization of suitable sites by these trees. Trees are indeed highly adapted for this, and their survival as successful competitive species depends on it. Anyone who has seen sycamore (*Acer pseudoplatanus*) seedlings flourishing on a heap of coke or sawdust will not need much convincing that, if man and all grazing animals were to be removed from England for a period of a hundred years, the whole country would again be covered with forest as it was in the distant past.

This ability to colonize what are, ecologically-speaking, vacant sites may help to explain the active dislike of sycamore by many conservationists. The high frequency with which it produces heavy crops of viable seed, and the distance over which these winged seeds can be carried by the wind, make it aggressive indeed. In circumstances in which oak (*Quercus* spp.) struggles to reproduce itself, there is obviously a considerable likelihood that a felled or decaying oakwood will rapidly be colonized by this virile tree. Those whose interest is in the perpetuation of oakwoods are apt in consequence to view it with alarm.

The virgin forests of the tropics and the more inaccessible parts of the Americas and Russian reproduce themselves by natural means, seedlings springing up wherever light is able to penetrate to the forest floor and whenever conditions are suitable for the production and germination of seed. The suggestion has been made that for every site there is a climax vegetation towards which constant movement is only interrupted from time to time by fire, flood, and pestilence. But while the site conditions — geological, edaphic, and biotic — remain constant, so according to this theory will there be a gradual ecological change back to the climax after such an interruption. While this is not now universally accepted as true, the principle is a simple one and the concept useful.

On the limestone soils of the Cotswolds, beech (*Fagus sylvatica*) would be the climatic climax; on the Oxford Clay to the east and on the Lias clays of the Severn valley, oak forest would develop. Development would be gradual with ash (*Fraxinus excelsior*), sycamore and birch (*Betula* spp.) acting as pioneer colonizers, certainly on the Cotswolds and probably also on the clays. This is because these trees are specially adapted for this purpose. The wings of the ash and sycamore seeds and the lightness of the birch (about 1800 seeds to one gramme) enable these trees to spread their progeny over a very wide area. Beech, however, is the most efficient tree on calcareous soils owing to its shade-bearing character which enables its seedlings to grow under, and come up through, the light shade cast by ash and birch. On the clays, oak has an advantage in its longevity and, though shorter-lived pioneers will occupy the clays at first, in the long run the forest will develop as relatively pure oakwood.

An interesting example of the way in which the natural spread of trees can occur was observed on a grassy ungrazed bank in the Cotswolds where an old and short-boled beech tree grew in isolation from other trees. With free growth it had produced a large and spreading crown. This old tree was surrounded by a complete belt of young oak trees, varying in width from five to 15 metres outwards from the very limits of the ground shaded by its crown. The interest of this example of colonization was greatly increased by the fact that the nearest oak seed-bearer was at least 500 metres distant. The agency for the carrying of acorns to this beech tree is assumed to have been birds, which probably means jays and possible pigeons, although the latter are unlikely to have released acorns from their crops unless shot while roosting. The suggestion that squirrels could have contributed seems very unlikely and mice and voles even more so. This is an interesting example when considered in isolation; but when the process is translated to a large area of virgin or unmanaged forest it opens up illuminating prospects of the ways in which a climax forest of oak evolves, despite the size and weight of the seed involved.

With the ability of trees to behave in this manner it may be asked why foresters do not make use of natural seeding to replace the trees that they cut for timber. The answer is, of course, that they do. But the harnessing of natural processes is rarely a simple matter, and natural regeneration, as it is known, is no exception. Silvicultural techniques based on natural regeneration are, however, in everyday use in France, Switzerland, Germany, and other European countries, as well as in India, Malaysia, parts of Africa, and elsewhere. They call for a thorough understanding not only of the individual tree and its behaviour but also of what might be called the 'group-behaviour' of the forest. They also require time.

Every species of tree has its peculiarities, and these must be understood if successful use is to be made of natural regeneration. The frequency with which a tree produces viable seed in quantity (seed- or mast-years) must be known. For instance, beech, which in southern England is growing at its north-western natural limit in Europe, produces a heavy general mast only once every 22 years, with a partial mast at intervals of 11 years. This is related to the sun-spot cycle since, in order to produce the necessary excess of sugar for flowering and seeding, this tree of warmer Continental Europe requires really hot sunny weather in the vital summer months. It is in July that the buds for the coming year are formed. If there is excess sugar being produced at this time owing to a very high rate of photosynthesis, then the buds formed will include a high proportion of flower-buds. If excess sugar is not present during these vital weeks then the new buds will be mainly of vegetative character, producing only leaves in the following year.

The irregularity of beech-masts in Britain — for not every 11-year interval produces a successful crop of seed — is due to a number of causes; the production of seed is only the first essential. An air-frost as the flowers appear in May might blight the crop before it developed and gales in autumn might bring down the unripe fruit. A high population of squirrels can reduce a crop locally and the fallen seed, if it escapes these perils, is avidly sought as food by a wide range of other mammals, birds, and insects.

To make practical use of natural regeneration, the manager must understand how such influences apply to the species under consideration. He must be aware of the ability of the seedlings of some species to withstand shade. For instance, although ash is light-demanding as a tree, its seedlings will stand quite heavy shade for several years before they finally disappear. The manager must know the method of seed-dispersal and the optimum size and shape of the crown for seed-production. For instance, in the classic French Uniform System the seeding-felling is of critical importance; it must be sufficiently heavy to permit the crowns to expand so that their flowers will be exposed to the sun, but not heavy enough to allow so much light to reach the ground that weed-growth is encouraged; and it must take place while the trees are still vigorous enough to respond and to produce heavy crops of seed. The manager must understand and make allowance for the ability of the fallen seed and the resultant seedlings to survive the attacks of mammal and insect pests, the reaction of the seed to the degree of acidity in the soil, and the seedling's ability to compete with ground vegetation; even the shape and size of the seed itself have to be taken into account.

An extreme example of a developed technique is offered by the method employed in the regeneration of pure maritime pine (*Pinus pinaster*) forest in the Landes, south of Bordeaux. Here the character of this pine makes it possible to dispense with the delicate manipulation of the forest canopy required in the oak and beech forests of northern and central France. Blocks of the pine forest are clear-felled and the brushwood spread evenly over the area after the timber has been removed. The cones, which are carried directly on the branches, open when exposed to the full heat of the sun and release their seeds. Natural regeneration follows, germination being assisted by the light shade of the brushwood.

A peculiarity that has been observed is that in uneven-aged forests of spruce (*Picea abies*) and silver fir (*Abies alba*) managed under the Selection System in France and Switzerland, it is found that silver fir seedlings appear more readily under spruce trees and vice versa. Another is that oak seedlings will often appear in thick grass, up to two kilometres from seed-bearing trees.

It is known that, as a general rule, conifer seedlings flourish in an acid medium. It is also commonly observable that weed-growth on acid soils is generally less luxuriant than on neutral or basic soils, and that seedlings thus have less competition to overcome. Which of these factors predominated in the case of seedlings of Atlas cedar (*Cedrus atlantica*) that the writer observed in the foothills of the Pyrenees germinating in the middle of a tarmac road might be open to question, had not the same species been seen germinating successfully at Vaucluse near Avignon in the middle of a path of bare limestone scree.

A matter of great importance to be considered when adopting natural regeneration methods is the quality of the trees available for producing seed, the seed-bearers. It is obviously unwise to depend on this method of reproducing tree crops if the resultant trees are likely to be badly-shaped, prone to low forking, or defective in any other particular. But the appearance of the parent trees may not necessarily be a reliable guide. There is no reason why physically crippled parents should not produce normal healthy children, or handsome parents produce idiots. It is the strain, the race of tree, that is important. We have therefore to distinguish between the genotypes, which transmit their physical characters to their offspring, and the phenotypes which have characters not passed on but which are the result of previous treatment, accident, or disease.

This is one of the principal arguments against the adoption of natural regeneration methods. If the stock can be improved simply by importing a certified good strain, it is obviously better to do this than to breed from inferior stock. To grow trees for 60, 100, or 120 years only to produce an inferior product would be absurd if it could be avoided by a little extra expense at the outset. On the other hand it should be remembered that the existing local stock has in all probability reached equilibrium with its environment, whereas an imported stock may be quite unsuited to it.

An example of poor parents producing good seedlings may be quoted from a sandy area in north Lincolnshire where a birchwood, heavily infested with rabbits, contained a few relic Scots pine (*Pinus sylvestris*) and larch (*Larix decidua*) from a previous crop that had been felled during the First World War. The pine had the appearance of decaying *bonzai*, with bent stems and broken limbs. When myxomatosis struck and the rabbit population was reduced to negligible proportions, pine seedlings began to appear and these were subsequently netted in and protected. The resultant crop, now some 40 years of age, is one of the nicest-looking areas of Scots pine to be seen anywhere, the product of unsightly parents of a good genotype.

These are just some of the problems and considerations to be taken into account when natural regeneration methods are used. These methods vary from straightforward techniques to complete and elaborate silvicultural systems. An example of the first is the planting of the scrub-covered hills of Provence with a few small groups of Atlas cedar in the 1860s. These were brought to France by a forest officer on leave from North Africa and planted at the western and windward end of Mont Luberon, a long limestone ridge extending to the east. These trees grew in exposed conditions, without competition or nurses, and developed into badly-shaped specimens, coarsely-branched. At 40 years of age they bore viable seed which dispersed downwind to the east, assisted by their efficient wings. This resulted in a good germination, the seedlings finding suitable conditions among the shrubs of the *garrigue* that sheltered and protected them. These seedlings flourished and, with the assistance of mutual shelter and favourable soil conditions, developed into fine straight trees like their ancestors; and they in turn produced seed in 1940. The trees that resulted from this seeding formed a dense crop 16 kilometres downwind from the original plantings when visited in the 60s. Their progeny will by now have spread perhaps another ten kilometres along the mountain. This is an excellent example of using natural seeding to establish pioneer crops.

It has been mentioned that for successful regeneration to appear the local site conditions must be absolutely right. The physical condition of the soil, including the overlying leaf-mould, and the height and species of shrubs, herbs, and grasses are critical to the germination of the seed and the establishment of the seedlings. It is these conditions that have given rise to the practice in irregular woods of 'following the regeneration'. The manager will find that, in a patch where full light or side light reaches the forest floor, a few seedlings have appeared and are growing with every appearance of health. This is his cue to increase the size of the opening by felling one or two trees on the north side of the gap and so to allow more light to reach these plants. They will respond; and at the same time the increased light experienced by the small area of the woodland floor immediately adjoining them will be brought into the same condition. The appearance of further seedlings can be expected with reasonable confidence. It is essential, however, that such progressive openings should be gradual; any over-extensive or over-rapid opening will change radically the micro-climate and micro-flora, and the chances of further regeneration will probably be lost. This is observed particularly with beech. Over-heavy opening of the canopy will encourage strong growth of bramble on many sites and of unfavourable grasses on others.

A characteristic of natural regeneration that has to be accepted is its comparatively slow rate of growth. Those who are accustomed to young plantations are often disappointed with the performance of natural seedlings. It is primarily this factor that accounts for the traditionally long regeneration period formerly employed in the French Uniform Shelterwood System. The reasons for the slower growth of the natural plant compared with that of the nursery-grown plant are partly environmental and partly physiological. The natural seedling grows where it falls and makes the best use it can of the conditions it finds. The cultivated seedling receives in its earliest stages the nearest to optimum conditions that the nurseryman can provide. The natural seedling puts out its roots and spreads them widely in search of the water and nutrients that it requires. The cultivated plant is provided with all the necessary nutrients in its immediate vicinity and has no need to expend energy in spreading its roots widely. Not only this, but the nurseryman deliberately prevents the production of such uneconomic lateral roots by under-cutting or transplanting, resulting in a compact root-system with a very much increased proportion of feeding-roots.

Where natural regeneration has appeared adventitiously (what is sometimes referred to as 'volunteer growth'), particularly in unmanaged or semi-derelict woodland, it will often be observed to form more or less pure groups. This is usually a reflection of the fact that a break has appeared in the woodland canopy due to the natural fall or death of a large tree at a time when adjoining trees were about to produce a crop of seed, or had indeed already produced seed. As the natural death of a tree is not normally a sudden occurrence but the final step of a protracted deterioration, changes in the ground flora below it are likely to be gradual, and a mixture of seedlings of several species may well appear. In the case of a tree uprooted by wind or broken by storm-damage, the increase of light experienced at ground-level will be sudden, and those trees in a position to exploit the opportunity will have the advantage. It is in such cases that pure groups will be likely to appear. Ash in particular is able to exploit such conditions owing to the fact that its seed normally remains dormant for one year before germinating. With a reasonable frequency of seed-years, therefore, there is always likely to be dormant seed in the ground awaiting just such an opportunity to colonize a gap. Both ash and sycamore seedlings are able to survive for several years under heavy shade, making minimal growth, before being finally shaded out; and such a 'bristle crop' is able, if given light, to advance from its entrenched position to take advantage of any new access of light.

A situation such as this can be manipulated to the advantage of the manager. An example may be drawn from a Herefordshire wood where a fine crop of ash, some 60 years of age, stood over sycamore coppice five to seven metres high. Normally it is almost impossible to regenerate ash under an ash crop because so much light passes through the canopy that there is invariably a very heavy growth of competing herbs. This is especially so on what is generally termed a 'good ash site'; that is, a deep moist loam. The situation is particularly frustrating where a fine crop of mature ash is involved since it is very important to ensure that the new crop will be of the same fine strain. In the case in point, the sycamore coppice gave dense shade, with the consequence that the soil was quite clear of growth other than a full complement of surviving ash seedlings, a few inches high. To regenerate that fine ash crop, all that was needed was to fell the sycamore coppice and to harvest the mature ash trees. The deliberate adoption of an under-storey of sycamore in a case like this would obviously be very well worthwhile.

The conditions required for the successful regeneration of beech in the Chiltern beechwoods were studied intensively by Ray Bourne during the period in the 1920s and 30s when he lectured and demonstrated in the sphere of forest management at the Department of Forestry at Oxford. His investigations showed considerable evidence of beech sickness in some of the woods where either coppicing or selective felling of beech had continued over a long period. The symptoms of this are well known and very obvious — dry, probably compacted, rendzina soils (thin soils over chalk), carrying little vegetation other than acid-indicating mosses, under a more or less dense crop of beech trees, generally of small girth and poor shape. These sites occur on shallow soils over chalk and are typical of exposed areas from which the leaf-litter has been removed by wind action. Mixture with other calcicole species, including wild cherry (*Prunus avium*), sycamore, ash, and whitebeam (*Sorbus aria*) not only improves the litter situation, but also allows the penetration of more light; this in turn encourages the growth of herbaceous plants which help to improve the soil and assist in holding the litter. In these conditions the establishment of natural regeneration at least becomes possible whereas under a dense, pure beech canopy this is unlikely to occur.

The accompanying diagram (Figure 1) was prepared by Bourne, and epitomises the conclusions he reached after some 20 years of field-work. It is based on the ecological system recognized in the 1930s, and shows how the ease or difficulty in obtaining successful natural regeneration of beechwoods is intimately associated with the permutations presented by geology, soil, and ground flora. Climate is not included; that of the chalk areas of southern England does not vary greatly, although micro-climate and aspect will vary from site to site. Drainage is implied in the soil types.

It will be seen that, in general, natural regeneration of beech is comparatively easy to obtain on rendzina soils carrying beech-ash-yew (*Taxus baccata*) woodland; on high pH brown-earths carrying beech-oak-ash woods; and on podsols and degraded brown-earths with a low pH in beech-oak-birch woodland.

Natural regeneration becomes difficult under beech-oak-ash where brown-earths with a pH of 5 to 7 are derived from flint-gravel; and also under beech-oak-birch where degraded brown-earths of pH 4 to 6 are derived from the whole range of parent material, from pebble-gravel to sands and clays. It becomes very difficult under beech-oak-ash on brown-earths of pH 5 to 7 derived from clay-with-flints, where the ground-flora consists mainly of bramble, woodrush, bluebell and sanicle.

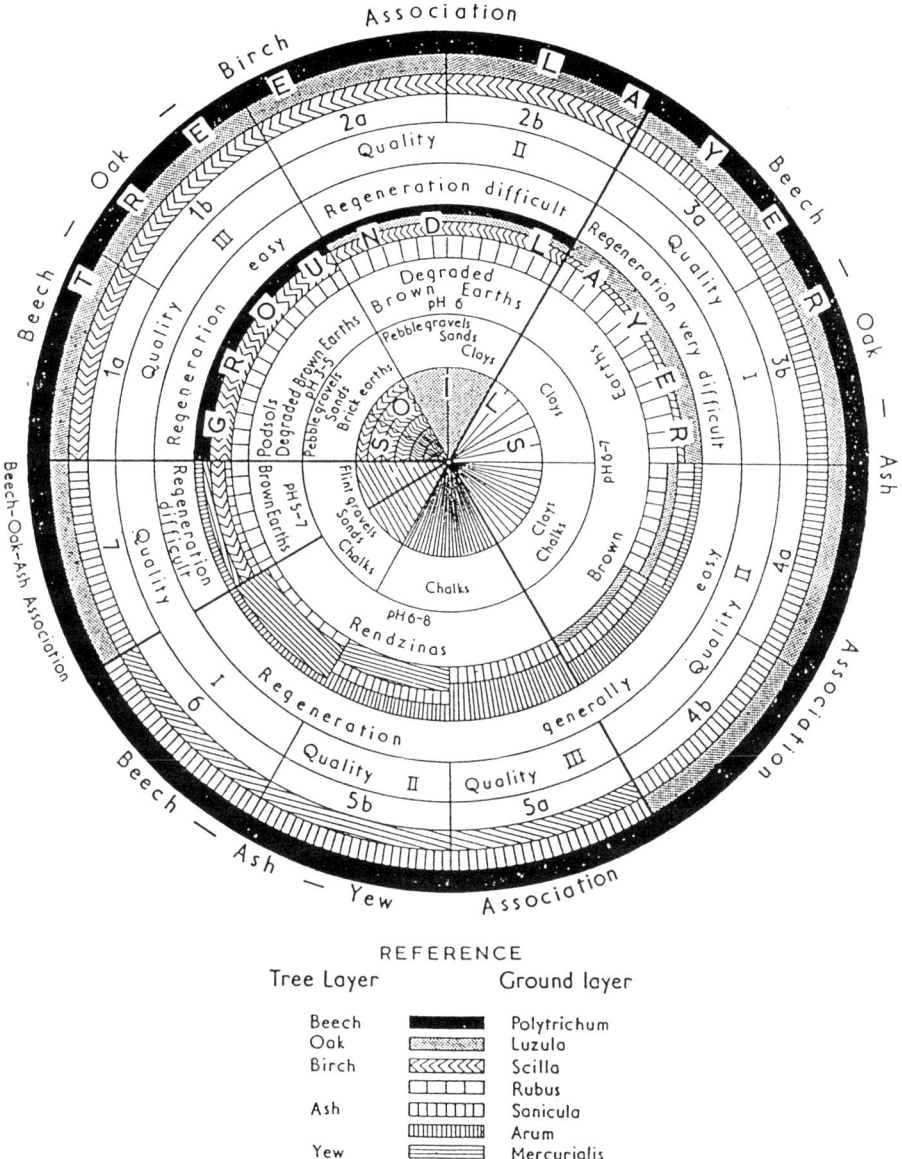

Figure 1. A key to beech (*Fagus sylvatica* L.) associations on chalk uplands in England. Devised by Ray Bourne. W.M. McNeill. *Forestry*, vol. XXXIV, no. 2, 1961

CHAPTER 3
Assisted Natural Regeneration

In addition to natural methods involved in manipulation of the forest canopy, natural regeneration can in some circumstances be induced artificially by mechanical means. A technique used on occasions in beech forest involves disturbance of the leaf-litter on the ground. Since the leaves of beech rot slowly, those that have fallen most recently form a carpet on which the seed lies exposed; not only exposed to the attention of pigeons, squirrels, and insects but also isolated by the still unrotted leaves from the underlying humus-layers and the mineral soil. The problem is therefore a dual one — to protect the seed from being eaten or destroyed before it can germinate, and to bring it into contact with the mineral soil. Unless both can be achieved, the chances of a satisfactory germination on a wide scale are small. It is essential that the young root should reach the mineral soil; to reach the layer of leaf-mould is not sufficient as this will not provide the vitally necessary supply of water and minerals for the short period during which the seedling is living on food stored in the cotyledons.

In many places on the Continent of Europe this necessary mixing of the organic and mineral layers is brought about by the activities of wild boar that trample the mast into the soil while feeding on it and while rooting in the organic layers for insects and earthworms. In mediaeval England the pannage of domestic swine in woods produced the same effect. Various artificial means have been devised to imitate this natural process in the absence of pigs.

One very effective system is to drag logs behind a tractor. Yew is preferred owing to its weight and to the toughness and durability of its branches. In this method three or four straight logs, about four metres long, are selected, and the branches removed in such a way as to leave branch-stubs of about 20 centimetres. The logs are attached by short chains to a tow-bar, with the butt-ends nearest to the bar. When towed over the forest-floor, the branch-stubs disturb the leaf-litter and the weight of the logs causes them to dig in deeply enough to bring up a proportion of mineral soil. The backward slope of the branch-stubs ensures that they do not produce an anchoring effect by jamming into obstructions such as old tree-stumps. There is a tendency for the logs to collect litter as they move forward but this is shed whenever they pass over an obstacle and by the semi-rolling action produced by the irregular setting of the branch-stubs. This method has been used by the author with very satisfactory results in beechwoods in the Cotswolds.

In France the same system was employed at one period, using a more formalized version in which round logs were utilized, with steel rods replacing branch-stubs. The latter were set at intervals and angles calculated to produce the best churning effect. In this way the logs could be made to rotate as they moved forward, swivels being provided to allow for this. However, in forest conditions it is doubtful whether the improved results in fact justified the added cost of production and liability to working failures.

As mechanization of agriculture has advanced, rotovators have also been used to achieve the same effect. But as is often the case, greater reliance on machines tends to produce problems of its own. The bigger the machine, the greater the compaction caused; and the more efficient the chopping of the litter layers, the greater the damage to surface-feeding roots and to any existing seedlings that may already be present. The yew-log system did no damage to surface-feeding roots and had no detrimental effect on patches of existing young seedlings over which the logs passed.

The great density of natural regeneration produces special problems, one being the intense root-competition. This is one of the main reasons for the slowness of growth referred to earlier. In Denmark it has been the practice to drive a brush-cutter through the dense masses of beech regeneration while it is still small enough for this to be possible. This results in a big reduction in the crop to be handled subsequently and cuts down the cost of the first cleanings.

A rather similar practice is in current use in French forests. This aims to reduce the dense natural seedling growth which results under the Uniform Shelterwood System by almost half. This is done by cutting parallel swathes through the growth, three to four metres wide, leaving standing belts between them. These are narrow enough to allow inspection to be made from the cleared tracks and to enable any cleaning or tending work to be done without difficulty. This method has the added advantage of providing easy access for machines and for fire-control.

From a silvicultural aspect the advantages of dense growth are retained in the belts, a sufficient stock is raised under intensive supervision to provide a full final crop, and the extraction of periodical thinnings is simplified.

Regeneration planting. A method combining natural regeneration and planting has been used on an estate in the Cotswolds. The soil consisted of 12 centimetres of clay over the platy limestone of the Oolite. The woods had been for a long time under oak coppice, with some ash and hazel, in which larch had been planted during the early years of this century. A few badly-shaped larches remained from this planting, along ride sides. It was in one of these old coppice areas that the experiments were started which led eventually to the complete re-stocking of a hectare block with a thriving crop of larch.

It is commonly observed that although conifers will regenerate freely on acid soils, their performance on calcareous soils is often poor. Occasional seedlings are found where there is no browsing by rabbits, hares, or deer; but the plants rarely survive the competition of herbaceous weeds and broad-leaved seedlings which grow strongly on these soils, casting heavy shade. In this wood rabbits, hares, and fallow deer were all present, and the usual calcicole herbaceous plants grew strongly. The owner had observed for some years that the old larches were producing good crops of seed which resulted in a scatter of seedlings; but these never appeared to increase significantly either in size or number. It was decided, therefore, to mark a number with sticks and, if necessary, to put protective sleeves round them. Observation soon showed that careful weeding and protection were resulting in the survival of a very large number of seedlings, all confined to a small area. To thin them out by destroying the surplus plants seemed to be wasteful, and the owner hit on the idea of transplanting them with a bulb-planter.

This proved to be suitable for very small seedlings but inadequate for the larger ones. An enlarged and modified bulb-planter was made and proved to be very efficient. This new version was circular in section, with a narrow gap at one side (see Figure 2). The tool was placed over the

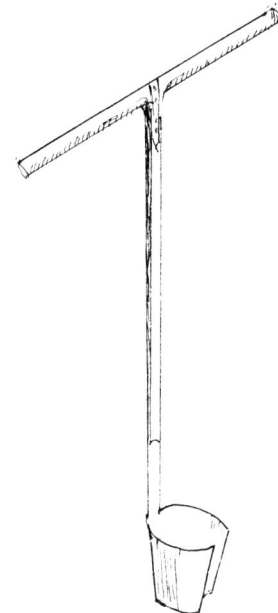

Figure 2. Modified bulb-planter

seedling and pressed into the ground with the foot. The handle was then twisted to rotate the tool, thus severing the block of soil at its base. The tool was then lifted vertically from the ground, together with the seedling securely held in its ball of soil. It was then carried to the replanting site, where a hole of exactly similar size had been made previously with the same tool. The tool containing the plant was placed in position in the hole and the plant with its ball of soil pressed out into it. This resulted in transplanting with almost complete absence of disturbance of the roots. With small seedlings, all the roots remained undamaged. In the case of larger plants the longer roots only were severed. The gap in the side of the planter allowed it to be used for plants up to 30 centimetres or more in height; the base of the stem was slipped through the gap, thus obviating the necessity for forcing the tool downwards over the side-branches.

Advantages claimed for this method of re-stocking old woodland were that the plants were of a strain known to be suited to the site; they grew away quickly since they had suffered no check on moving; there was no damage to the root-systems; planting could be done at any time of the year; and natural seedlings of this kind were found to be less susceptible to grazing by deer than introduced plants. In addition, the plants did not have to be brought in from a nursery and so were not subject to drying-out or any of the hazards involved in lifting and transplanting.

One of the arguments against the use of natural regeneration is that the manager is confined to the provenance or race of tree already growing on the site; he cannot improve his stock. If this is poor, it is obviously undesirable to breed from it. However, trees of superior provenance (or of other species) can be introduced into existing beds of dense ash, sycamore, and birch regeneration by the simple expedient of clearing small individual patches and planting in tree-shelters. In this way they are provided with natural conditions of density, with a ready-made ecological environment. The existence of the plastic shelter is a sufficient means of identification when the time comes for the introduced tree to be given more space.

Similarly and more cheaply, the bud-grafting of a very small proportion of ash and sycamore stems in dense stands of regeneration is a possibility for the future. Trials may well show the feasibility of reproducing male ash of high quality and rippled ('fiddle-back') sycamore by this means.

CHAPTER 4

Natural Regeneration Systems in Even-Aged Woods

The systems by which forests are managed in the long term are known as silvicultural systems. They provide for the establishment, tending, removal and replacement of tree crops on a continuing basis; and each system results in stands with special characteristics. It is convenient at this stage to consider those systems that produce even-aged woods or forests. These are often referred to in general terms as 'regular' systems.

Although there are many woods in Britain that may be classed as ancient and of semi-natural origin, it is probable that the majority today bear crops that were established artificially in part and many can be seen to consist of trees of approximately the same age. Younger woods, which do not fall into these categories, are axiomatically of plantation origin. All these, for our immediate purpose, can be classed as even-aged woods. Together they constitute by far the largest proportion of our British woodlands, and their perpetuation presents very real problems.

Until comparatively recently, in terms of a tree's life, it has been customary in these islands to treat woods in the same manner as agricultural crops. That is to say, the owners cut a wood down when it was considered to be mature or when money was required for some specific purpose, and they subsequently replanted it. This was the normal procedure, the replanting being considered essential on a well-managed estate; for virtually all woodland formed part of an estate belonging either to the Crown, one of the colleges of the old universities, or to some other large landowner. The woodlands formed an integral part of such estates, frequently constituting the setting of some great house. Only in exceptional circumstances would the replanting of a felled wood be deliberately neglected.

With the opening-up of the countryside that has followed the widespread use of the motor-car and the consequent enormously expanded interest of the country's largely urban population in the conservation of every cherished visual aspect, clear-felling no longer appears as an acceptable option. The public know what they like to see and, through the agency of a multiplicity of interested bodies, they have the power to make their preferences known. Society as a whole accepts that violent changes to beautiful and familiar landscapes are undesirable.

There is a built-in problem arising from these attitudes, due to the exceptionally long life of a woodland crop — for by far the majority of woods are expected to produce some money in due course — and the exceptionally short memory of the public. This is well illustrated by the experience of a well-known landowner in west Gloucestershire who had inherited a larch plantation on the lower side of a hill road. As the plantation came to maturity and the increment began to fall off, the landowner felled it as a routine exercise, selling the timber and crediting the proceeds to the estate accounts. This was regarded by the local residents as an act of vandalism. This beautiful wood that they had known and admired all their lives had been cut down by a greedy landowner for money; it was disgraceful. However, nothing could be done about it; in those days there were no statutory powers to control a woodland-owner's activities. Nevertheless, being a good and provident manager, the owner replanted the wood as soon as the timber was cleared and in due course the outcry died down.

Now, in felling the plantation a wide view over valleys and hills had been opened up to people passing along the road. After some 15 years the newly-planted larch trees began to appear over the top of the roadside wall and soon formed a complete screen above it. Feeling began to rise in the area that the beautiful view that the local residents had known and admired all their lives was now denied to them by the money-grubbing activities of this grasping landowner.

The emphasis therefore is likely to be placed increasingly on methods of perpetuating the woodland landscape, and so the woodlands themselves, by methods other than clear-felling and planting. For a full range of the options open we turn to the Continent of Europe where systematic forest management has been in practice for centuries. The French Service des Eaux et Forêts was in fact inaugurated by Colbert, Minister of Marine to Louis IV, in 1630, in order to safeguard the supply of ship-building timber. Germany and Switzerland also have a long history of systematic forest management which, if not as impressively early as that of France, precedes our own Forestry Commission by well over 100 years.

In none of the silvicultural systems practised on the Continent of Europe does truly even-aged woodland as understood in Britain really exist. The Continental European systems were devised, or rather developed gradually, as a result of the need to handle in an effective manner very large tracts of forest. The object generally was to produce at regular intervals a more or less constant supply of wood for national needs, without reducing the forest area and therefore capital represented by the trees. This concept is known to professional foresters as *sustained yield* and can best be explained by the example of a forest of 100 hectares, growing on a rotation of 100 years, one hectare being felled and replanted each year in perpetuity.

But planting was an activity that was rarely resorted to in these Continental European forests and the reasons are not far to seek. As mentioned above, the areas to be dealt with nationally were very large indeed and the forest services consisted of a relatively small cadre of highly-skilled officers. The money for the detailed work of planting and tending young plantations simply was not available. As trees in reasonably favourable conditions are able to reproduce themselves by seed, this ability was exploited by various techniques. All the best-known Continental European systems of silviculture were therefore based on the assumption that the forest, properly handled, would reproduce itself if given time. This was expressed in the saying of the old French forest service that they had a sufficiency of land, a sufficiency of time, but no money. The range of options for regenerating a forest on the Continent of Europe is wide, but the applicability of these systems to British forestry is limited by at least two of the factors referred to. Britain does not possess large blocks of forest comparable to those of our European neighbours, and indeed the proportion of our total forest area to that of the whole of Great Britain, is under ten per cent, compared with 27 per cent in France. So we do not have a sufficiency of land for large-scale silvicultural systems. Nor do we have unlimited time. Whereas the classic Uniform Shelterwood System in France allows a period of from 15 to 40 years within which regeneration is expected to be completed out of a total rotation of between 120 and 160 years, in Britain the Forestry Commission expects a crop to be re-established on felled ground in considerably less than ten years.

The direct implication is that silvicultural systems with a more or less even-aged crop of trees, and based on natural regeneration, are not a practical option for British woodlands. This at a blow rules out the Uniform Shelterwood System, which is widely used in beech and oak forests in France and is operated through the phased removal of the over-crop as natural seedlings spread over the forest-floor. As the trees approach maturity, occasion is found to open up the canopy to allow light to reach all parts of the upper crowns of the largest trees. This stimulates flowering, and is known as the seeding-felling. Once seed begins to be produced in suitable quantities, the crop is opened up by stages to allow adequate light to reach the new seedlings, while retaining sufficient shelter to protect them. The final felling involves the removal of all the remaining seed-bearers when the area is fully re-stocked with seedlings.

The result is a crop of trees varying in age over the regeneration period; that is to say, with a 40-year regeneration period the oldest trees will be 40 and the youngest one year old. By the end of the rotation of, say, 160 years it will have the appearance of an even-aged crop. This harmonizing effect will be accentuated in later years as regular thinnings remove the poorer and suppressed trees. On the other hand, a proportion of the latter are deliberately retained to assist with the shading-out of weeds on the forest-floor, a most important requirement as a preliminary to the next seeding-felling.

Only variants of systems in which planting is substituted for natural regeneration can be employed widely in Britain, although of course any regeneration that occurs can be used to reduce the planting that is necessary. This conclusion refers to the generality of woodlands but does not apply to individual estates where local circumstances have made it possible to regenerate some species with success, as has been done with Scots pine on the sandy soils of the Crown Estate at Windsor. There, after felling, the site is bulldozed clear to expose the soil in which the pine seed

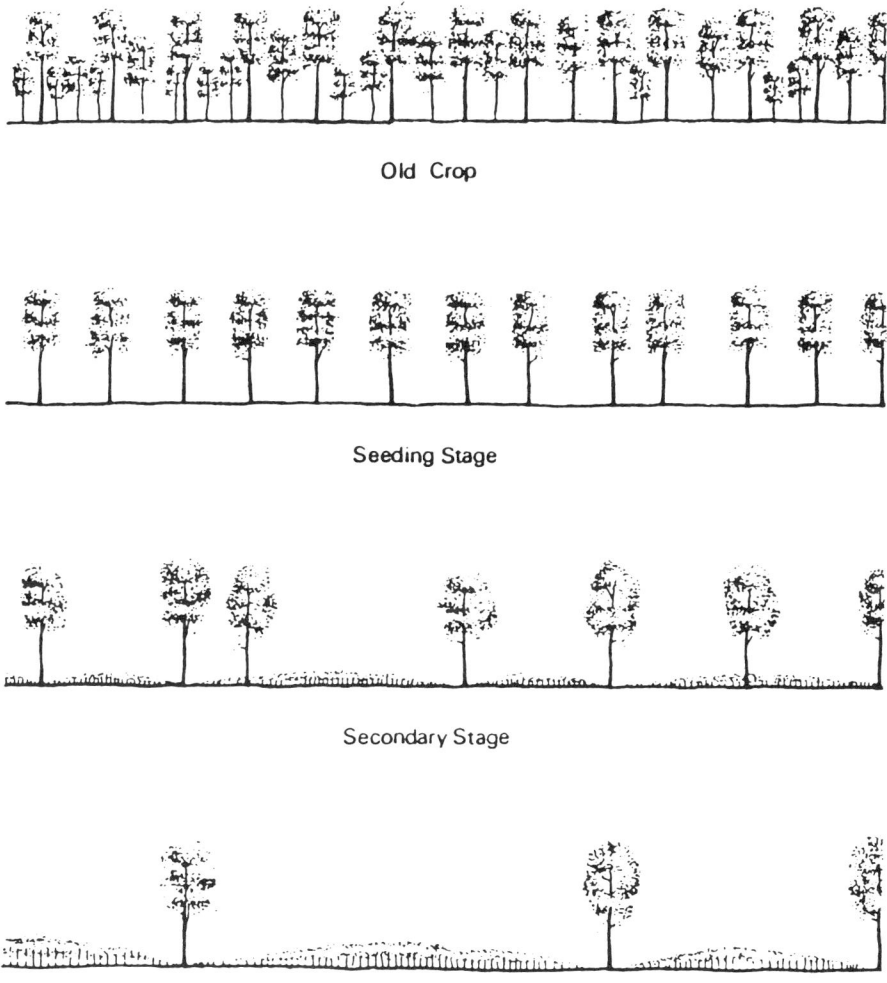

Figure 3. Uniform Shelterwood System, showing successive stages of regeneration in beech.

finds optimum conditions for germination and complete freedom from competition by herbaceous weeds and grass. This procedure can be applied only in comparatively small individual areas that can be reached by seed from neighbouring pine stands; and the extent of the clear-fellings is limited by this factor.

CHAPTER 5

Natural Regeneration Systems in Irregular Woods: Coppice-with-Standards

This system, in which both standard timber-trees and coppice are grown on the same piece of ground, is the oldest form of irregular forestry. Although still in use on the Continent of Europe, it is not well understood in Britain. To many people a coppice-with-standards wood is one in which branchy oak trees stand above a more or less dense crop of hazel (*Corylus avellana*) coppice. And since they have been told that the system has been in operation for many hundreds of years, the impression has gained ground that mediaeval woodlands were of this character. The evidence indicates that this is far from being the case.

The best examples of coppice-with-standards today can be seen in France where the system is still widely practised. There too the standards are principally oak, but the coppice is mainly oak, ash, sweet chestnut (*Castanea sativa*), alder (*Alnus glutinosa*), sycamore, or other minor species capable of producing firewood or other products of medium dimension.

Our hazel coppices in England mostly derive from a combination of the patterns of our agriculture and our field-sports. During the improvement era of the 18th and 19th centuries many woods were planted with oak and hazel in south and south-east England. Hazel grows quickly and produces dense cover; its periodical cutting results in glades distributed over the woodland area, and this provides successive open shooting stands, close low nesting cover for pheasants and dense protective shelter. For the farmer it provided, until comparatively recently, perennial crops of hurdle-stakes, stakes and heathers for laying hedges, spekewood or thatching-spars for houses and ricks, as well as beansticks and peasticks, and faggots for the bread-oven.

But in earlier times, before the development of modern methods of pheasant-shooting, the woodland was called upon to grow all the fuel required, not only by the local villages but also by the neighbouring towns. It takes a long time for hazel to produce useful firewood and even after 15 or 20 years the proportion on each stool is small. Ash and oak were the principal trees that were coppiced for this purpose and on suitable rotations they also produced small-sized timber for farm-buildings and for the craftsmen of the village — coopers, wheelwrights, and carpenters — as well as charcoal for the smith.

Except for peat in the moorland areas and coal in the Forest of Dean and the north-east, wood was the only available fuel in early times, and a continuous supply was essential on a sustained yield basis as coppice. It was required all the year round for cooking as well as for warmth in winter, and the demand was very large. Firewood was as necessary to life as food itself.

Timber was required for what may be called capital projects; the frames of houses and, on occasions, for the building of bridges and churches. There was constant work for the carpenter and wheelwright. Since transport was difficult when there were still no hard roads and navigable rivers were few and far between, it was essential that both fuel and timber should be easily accessible. This gave rise to the compromise of growing both timber and coppice-wood on the same ground, and their development into the classic coppice-with-standards system. There are records of an early form as far back as AD 600 in Germany; it was a recognized system in France by the year 1200 and references to its use in the English midland counties are found from 1295 onwards.

Of course there was also a parallel demand for small coppice wood for fencing needs, as well as for the wattle used for filling in the spaces between the heavy wooden frames of buildings — the familiar wattle-and-daub — and the multitude of craft uses. But the weight of material used by the village for these purposes would be very small indeed in comparison with the weight of fuel burnt by the inhabitants during the same period. The writer's experience shows that one modest wood fire, burning only in the evenings from early autumn to late spring, requires two tonnes of dry firewood a year. A small village of 30 households would, on this basis, require 60 tonnes of fuel a year. The requirement is in fact likely to have been very much higher since the two tonnes quoted served only for the heating of one room, without any cooking.

Calculations based on figures taken from one of the forestry manuals, and assuming a rotation for oak standards of 100 years with 20 years for coppice, show that branchwood from the standards felled would amount to about 37 tonnes on one hectare at each coppice-fall. Thus, if only branchwood from standards were available, the village would need to fell a 1.6-hectare coupe each year. With a rotation for the standards of 100 years, the area of woodland required would be 160 hectares. Even without the extravagance of such a large area of forest to provide the fuel requirements of such a small settlement, the transport of the wood over the distances implied is likely to have been beyond the means of the inhabitants in the absence of surface roads. From these considerations it becomes obvious that the principal source of firewood lay in the coppice-with-standards wood; and that it was species other than hazel that supplied this firewood.

Much of the hazel required would be obtained from growth at woodsides — a typical site — in full sunlight, and from the cutting and laying of such hedges as existed. Indeed it was the practice until quite recently for the stakes and heathers required in the laying of hedges to be obtained from the hedge itself, by selecting suitable pieces of material during the necessary preliminary thinning-out process. There were also, of course, special areas devoted entirely to the production of pure coppice, especially for hazel and willow where there was a demand for straight wands. Hazel grown in this way in full sunlight will produce more usable straight shoots more quickly than when grown in the partial shade of heavily-branched standards. The words 'coppice' and 'withybed' occur regularly on woodland estates, and the word 'springs' generally also refers to coppice. Coppice grown under standards is known generally as 'underwood'. The species of which it is composed are those that will produce both valuable timber as standards and a plentiful supply of firewood when grown as coppice. Oak was the most important tree grown in the wood, not only because the framework of most buildings were made of its timber on account of its durability but also because oak has a higher calorific value than any other native wood, with the possible exception of yew. It is hard and heavy and gives out greater heat, and thus when dry makes the most efficient firewood. It is easy to work in large dimension because of the facility with which it can be split. This characteristic made it possible to split sizeable tree-trunks of suitable shape to make the main matching timbers of what are known as 'cruck houses', and to split billets into clefts that were woven into panels for use instead of hazel wattles in building construction. Examples of this technique can still be seen in houses and farm-buildings in Herefordshire.

Ash was almost equally important. Although not durable in contact with the soil, it was widely used in the manufacture of farming implements owing to its flexible character. But its importance lay primarily in the rapidity with which it grew when coppiced and the weight of material that it produced. Ash makes fine fuel, traditionally 'fit for a queen', and there is little doubt that it provided the greater part of the village's household requirements in this respect. Also, every bit of it could be used, the long clean poles growing from the stools providing the wide-ringed springy wood for axe-hafts and handles of every kind, as well as hurdle-stakes and hedge-stakes. Timber from the standard trees was ideal for the construction of waggons to be used over uneven ground, standing up to the strain better than any other wood. Owing to the frequency with which ash produces seed and the efficiency with which it is distributed by the wind, there would be no shortage of this very important tree.

Sweet chestnut, which has been an important local constituent of English woodland since its introduction in Roman times, also coppices with great vigour, and produces long straight poles and timber-lengths from its stools. It was used as a substitute for oak in some areas, probably owing to the longer, clean lengths that were obtainable. An example of its use is in the half-timbered Market House at Ledbury in Herefordshire; and it is probable that many old 'oak' buildings would prove to be chestnut if the timbers were subjected to detailed examination. Its coppice provides good stakes — more durable than larch, even — for fencing, and sticks of all kinds.

In the 13th and 14th centuries lime (*Tilia* spp.), hornbeam (*Carpinus betulus*), and elm (*Ulmus* spp.) are recorded as having been used; and beech, birch, and aspen (*Populus tremula*) are referred to in the 18th century. Hazel is recorded in the past as having been specifically removed from some oak coppices in Cornwall and also in Scotland. In Surrey in

1813 sallow (*Salix caprea*), ash, alder, willow (*Salix alba*), oak, chestnut and maple (*Acer campestre*) were listed in coppices.

All these species would find a niche in the coppice-with-standards coupes but certain species were essential to the system of management. As practised on the Continent of Europe, coppice-with-standards is operated as follows. The forest area is divided into a number of coupes, the rotation being fixed according to the age at which the coppice will be cut, which in turn will depend on the size of the produce required. Ideally, in each block of forest there will be as many coupes as there are years in the rotation so that one coupe will be cut each year. When a coupe is due for attention the coppice is first cut clear. A number of standards are felled; and a number of the new maiden trees that have become established since the last cutting of the coppice are retained to grow on. Blanks caused by the felling of standards are filled up, either by natural regeneration or planting. The result of these operations is that, after the system has been in operation for a sufficiently long period, there will be a range of standards with ages representing multiples of the coppice rotation (r); thus r, 2r, 3r, 4r, etc.

The number of standards to be retained will depend on the relative importance given to the timber and the coppice. The greater the proportion of standards, the less will be the vigour of the coppice, due to shading. A normal figure will probably be between 50 and 100 standards to the hectare. In order to ensure that there will be a sufficiency of good young standards, known as 'tellers', more of the very young ones will be retained than are actually required, and the numbers will be gradually reduced by careful thinning at each successive felling of the coppice. Thus of the 100 standards on one hectare, there may be, say, 50 of age r (just recruited), 30 of 2r, 20 of 3r, and 10 of age 4r (due for felling as timber).

Standards should ideally be of seedling origin, but in the absence of a sufficient supply of these maidens, suitable young coppice-shoots may be selected for retention. These must be straight shoots springing from a point close to the ground on the outside at the lower limit of the stool. From this position the shoot, as it grows, will make its own root-system instead of relying on that of the stool. The old stool, which will be small since it will have been selected with this in mind, will eventually be incorporated in the base of the new standard. Oaks treated in this way can usually be identified on reaching timber-size by the fact that on one side the tree is flat and appears to grow vertically out of the ground, while on the other there is a

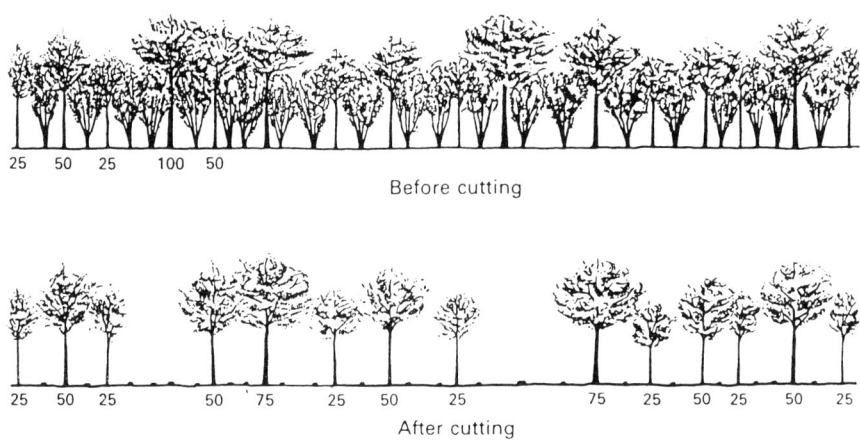

Figure 4. Coppice-with-standards, before and after cutting. Rotation of coppice 25 years; rotation of standards 100 years. Numbers denote ages of standards

clearly-seen buttress. With tellers of coppice-origin it is generally necessary in the early stages to remove any surplus secondary shoots that may arise from the same stool.

Since coppice grows with greater vigour than seedlings, the young tellers may well require assistance during their early years to keep them free from damage by competing coppice. But once the danger period is past, no further attention should be necessary unless pruning appears to be called for. This may include the removal of epicormic shoots that appear when rotational cutting of the coppice allows more light to fall on the stems.

With the increasing attention now being given to broad-leaved woodland there will inevitably be more interest in coppice-with-standards, and it is important that its operation should be fully understood. Its advantage, at times when there is a strong demand for wood fuel and hardwood pulp, is that it produces early returns from cutting the coppice. From the conservation point of view the system is preferable to simple coppice since it combines permanent protection of the soil, which is never fully exposed, with preservation of the ground flora and the habitat for wildlife. On the amenity side, both the overall appearance of the wood and the shelter it gives remain unaltered. From the point of view of private occupiers, the system provides good cover for game. Some authorities claim that coppice-with-standards woods carry a smaller forest capital than most forms of high forest, and that it is flexible and can be increased or decreased without affecting the operation of the system.

Unmanaged woodland, where there is a fair distribution of trees and coppice of all sizes, intimately mixed, can be converted to a coppice with-standards condition by the following method. First, a decision must be made as to the relative importance of the coppice and of the standards, and on this the number of standards of each age, or size-class, to be retained will be determined. These standards are then selected and marked, and everything else is felled. If the rotation for coppice is 25 years and that for standards is 100 years, the number and assumed age (estimated from the diameter) of the standards to be retained in this initial operation will be approximately 37 of 25 years, 23 of 50 years, and 15 of 75 years. The state of the wood will, in fact, resemble an existing coppice-with-standards crop immediately after a rotational cutting during which the oldest standards have been harvested. The youngest standards will be aged 25 years; but the new seedlings now germinating (or in their absence, plants) will be on the ground and will be growing on, to be aged 25 years at the next cutting. The standards will reach maturity at 100 years, when they will probably be two in number. This distribution will remain constant, the numbers of the standards in each class being progressively reduced by thinnings at the end of each coppice rotation.

Coppice-with-standards is a system that can offer real attractions to a woodland owner at the present time, but only if properly handled. Conservation groups proposing to embark on this system should ensure that they have competent professional advice, since attempts to operate it with insufficient understanding, particularly if the existing coppice element is hazel, are likely to result in disappointment and heavy expense. Hazel is not a profitable crop and the rotational cutting and removal of the underwood will be a heavy charge on the management.

CHAPTER 6

Natural Regeneration Systems in Irregular Woods: the Selection System

The Selection System is known in France as *jardinage*. The concept of the system is totally different from the clear-cutting and planting that has been the practice almost universally applied in Britain, at least since the establishment of the Forestry Commission in 1919. There is no clear-cutting and no planting in this system. The whole forest is totally irregular; that is to say, trees of all sizes exist together on the same site. Felling is by individual trees, and re-stocking is by seed dropped by the mature specimens. The effect of the application of the system is to produce an uneven crop of trees that never alters in overall appearance or structure. It is a simple concept, belied by the minutiae of management.

In theory only mature trees are removed and then only when they have grown to a pre-determined exploitable size, which is usually expressed in terms of the diameter. In practice, however, periodical thinnings are required in addition, not only to remove badly-shaped or otherwise unsuitable trees, but also to reduce the numbers of the younger trees as they increase in size. This will be obvious when it is remembered that natural regeneration over a recently opened area may mean perhaps hundreds of seedlings to a square metre; whereas one mature tree may itself have a crown diameter of ten metres or more.

Since trees of all sizes are growing intimately mixed together and there is no date of planting, the seeding being more or less continuous, the

Figure 5. Selection System. Profile in conifer forest

concept of age is abandoned and size becomes the criterion by which management is effected. Rotation, as applied to even-aged systems, ceases to have any meaning. The Selection System has been refined to a high degree in France and Switzerland, both from the silvicultural and from the management angles. It requires intensive supervision and skill in operation, not only from the cultural aspects but also in controlling the volume of timber to be removed, and in harvesting.

Since the continued existence of the forest depends entirely on natural regeneration, every new group or patch of seedlings must be allowed to grow wherever there is light to encourage it. This means that aggressive woody weed species such as sallow and birch must be eliminated, and woody climbers meticulously cut back or removed. Only suitable tree species can be accepted as components of the crop, and the choice is limited to tolerant or shade-bearing species, particularly beech, silver fir and spruce.

In the harvesting of exploitable trees and marketable thinnings, great skill is required in the felling and extraction to avoid damage, both to patches of regeneration and to the surrounding trees of all sizes. With the adequate provision of rides and roads, skilled and experienced operators can reduce damage to a minimum. Some clearing and exposure of the soil is inevitable during these operations, and this provides opportunities for the establishment of new seedling regeneration.

The ultimate *theoretical* aim of the Swiss foresters is that one seedling should produce one middle-sized tree that should develop into one exploitable tree. With this in mind, techniques have been devised to control the way in which the forest develops. The manager requires to know at any moment how the crop is constituted; what proportion of it is composed of large trees, smaller trees, saplings, and seedling regeneration. This is necessary in order that at each felling he can remove the correct proportion of each size-class to ensure the steady growth of the forest at its highest potential. This involves intricate calculations which must be based on accurate data. The necessary information has in the past been obtained by detailed enumeration of all the trees in the forest at regular intervals; more recently various forms of sampling have been employed since the high cost of labour now makes complete enumeration prohibitively expensive.

A sampling method that was used on a Chiltern estate near Princes Risborough was based on an intensive regional survey completed some years previously. This enabled a line-transect to be employed. Lines were drawn on a large-scale map at right-angles to the change of geological outcrops and topography, cutting through the boundaries of the surveyed regions. These were then demarcated on the ground and all the trees in a belt 20 metres wide along them were measured. Callipers were used to record diameters; and the point of measurement on each tree was marked with a scribe so that all subsequent measurements could be made at the same point. This enabled a subjective estimate of the volume of the sample to be calculated. Although it might not result in a strictly accurate figure for the standing volume when applied to the whole wood, it did provide a basis on which two successive measurements could be compared to give an accurate estimate of the increment. At the same time it provided the essential information concerning the distribution of the size-classes.

One of the special features of the Selection System, when beech and silver fir are used, is that there is a sharing of space. The strong shade-bearing character of these species allows young trees to develop below the crowns of older trees, provided only that there is adequate side light; light from a point vertically above is not necessary. The result is that there will be more trees growing on a given area with this system than would be the case with an even-aged system where there is no sharing of space. This fact has led to claims that a higher increment per unit of area can be obtained by the employment of the Selection System.

Another special feature arises from the same observation. A tree growing in partial shade will have narrow annual rings in the early stages of its growth. When it is opened up to full light, although the annual increment of wood will be greater, this will be distributed over an increasingly larger core, resulting again in reduced ring-width. The overall result therefore will be timber with more or less consistently narrow rings. In the case of trees in an even-aged system, which always enjoy full light, the opposite is the case; rapid growth on a small core produces wide rings which become progressively narrower as the tree grows and the core becomes larger. Thus a tree experiencing early shading will tend to produce timber of more even grain, and so of better quality, than one grown on a regular system.

The Selection System does not work so well in pure beechwoods with no mixture of silver fir, which does not thrive in Britain where it suffers from severe attack by an aphid. Nevertheless there are examples still to be seen in the Chilterns where it was formerly a widely-used traditional method. It was rarely operated with the skill found in France and Switzerland, however, and the crude removal of the largest trees with little management of the smaller sizes has led over the centuries to a general deterioration of the woodland. In fact it has been found in some places that the smaller trees in a wood that was believed to be uneven-aged were actually no younger than their larger companions, their small size being merely a reflection of the fact they had never enjoyed full light. These crops were in fact even-aged. These woods had not been managed under the Selection System; they had been 'selectively-felled', a very different matter.

A formalized version of the Selection System was developed by the late Lord Bradford on his property near Tavistock in Devon. In this he made full use of all possible shade-bearing timber trees, especially western red cedar (*Thuja plicata*), with very promising results. There is no reason why western red cedar, together with Lawson cypress (*Chamaecyparis lawsoniana*) of a suitable non-forking race, and perhaps Douglas fir (*Pseudotsuga menziesii*) should not be used successfully with beech in Britain. Indeed, the Selection System can of course be operated with conifers alone.

From an environmental angle the principal advantages of the Selection System are that a constant forest cover is maintained, resulting in a minimum exposure of the soil; and from this follows protection from erosion. At the same time, damage from wind and snow is minimized since individual trees are at no time subjected to sudden exposure. Any small local damage resulting from wind is easily incorporated into the working of the forest, the openings caused in this way being similar to those made deliberately to free seedling regeneration.

Beech seed-years tend to be infrequent in Britain but this is no great disadvantage under the Selection System since seed-years occurring at any time can be taken advantage of; and the seedlings are well protected. In addition, the system is very flexible and intensive, with the result that the best possible use can be made of individual sites and the productive capacity of the soil can be conserved.

From a management angle there is no need to keep such a high proportion of young trees to old ones as in forest with a regular canopy where there must be equal areas of each age-class. So, therefore, a larger proportion of the growing-stock and timber yield can be in the form of large trees of high value. It is also possible to retain individual stems of good form and to allow them to grow on as long as they are putting on valuable increment; they need not necessarily be felled merely because they have reached a certain age, as in the case of regular woods. Age indeed is immaterial, only size being considered. Because the crowns of the largest trees are well developed and unrestricted by those of near neighbours, they continue to put on increment at a useful rate to an advanced age.

The large crowns resulting from free growth produce butt-lengths of large girth and high quality. These are the most important part of the tree and this results in the whole stem being more valuable than those of longer length and smaller girth, much of the length of the latter being the crown, knotty, and of less value.

Where amenity is an important consideration, the Selection Forest is attractive, its appearance never seeming to change. Its advantages from a conservation point of view are self-evident. The principal disadvantages of the system are that it can only be operated with shade-bearing species and that it depends on the effective control of deer, rabbits and squirrels. In this latter respect it is no different from all the other systems of forest management.

CHAPTER 7

Natural Regeneration Systems in Irregular Woods: the Group Selection System

Beech is a shade-bearing species but it responds strongly to light in normal circumstances, and ill-formed stems tend to be produced in the absence of adequate light at the critical seedling stage. This leads inevitably to the adoption of heavier openings in selection forest, resulting in groups of more or less even-aged regeneration.

The deliberate creation of groups is a natural development; in the case just considered this is for the freeing of young seedlings appearing at the base of mature trees. It may also be done in order to establish other, less tolerant, species. At this point the true Selection System develops into the Group Selection System. The overall aims of the two systems are the same, namely the maintenance of permanent cover of an irregular character over the whole forest area. Operating by groups makes it possible to employ a wide variety of species, irrespective of their tolerant or intolerant character as regards shade, thus allowing full weight to be given to their natural preferences as to soil type, depth, and drainage.

Since it is of the essence of the system that the trees should be allowed to grow in full light, the groups must be of a certain minimum size; this is sometimes defined as having a diameter at least one and a half times the height of the surrounding crop. It is probable that in most conditions and on most soils in England and Wales the optimum size will be between 0.3 and 0.9 of a hectare. Except where total reliance is placed on natural regeneration, the distribution of the species within such groups is entirely under the control of the manager.

Since the groups consist of more or less even-aged trees, the distribution of the age- or size-classes throughout the forest is determined by the groups, which take the place of individual stems in the true Selection System. In the latter there is a theoretical spread of size-classes from seedling to exploitable tree, although in fact for control purposes these are reduced to four or five by combining them into super-classes. In Group Selection, unless the forest being managed is of very large extent, it is convenient to avoid small fellings and plantings and to space them out at intervals of five or ten years. It will be clear that the choice of this cycle will determine the extent of the felling that is to be carried out in one year. This will be made up of a number of groups. Thus if the 'rotation' (in this context, the time required for a tree to reach exploitable size) were to be 120 years in the case of oak and the felling-cycle five years, then one twenty-fourth of the total area would be felled and re-stocked every five years; or, if ash and sycamore were to be grown on a 60-year 'rotation', one twelfth of the area would be felled and re-stocked on the same cycle.

There are considerable advantages in this method of management since control is by area and not by volume (size-classes), as is inevitable with the true Selection System. It is thus possible to work to strict sustained principles without the necessity for labour-intensive periodical enumerations; and this can be specially important in circumstances where ownership is by a public body and where any suggestion of over-cutting of timber can be clearly refuted. The flexibility of the system is one of its great advantages, since it allows local deviations in the form of the retention of an occasional group of particularly fine trees to an age beyond the normal, or the introduction of new species, or even the limited production of Christmas trees.

Harvesting problems are reduced by the fact that, although the coupes are small, the actual operation is a limited clear-fall. Normal careful felling is therefore sufficient, without the need for exceptional skill such as is required in operating the true Selection System. For each group felled there need be only one tractor-wide track through the neighbouring forest to the nearest ride or road. Liability to wind-damage is reduced by the fact that the canopy is constantly exposed to wind and remains stable when adjoining groups are felled.

Figure 6a. Group Selection System. Rotation 100 years; felling-cycle 20 years. Profile immediately prior to felling of the 100-year-old group

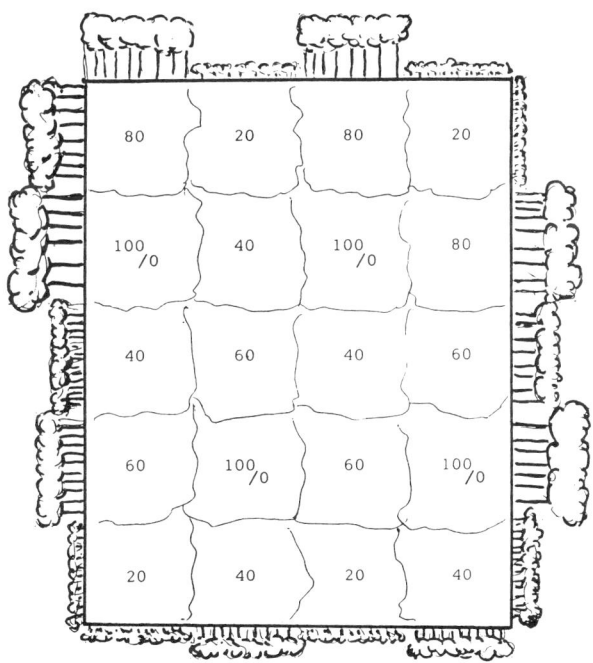

Figure 6b. One of the many possible patterns in group selection forest, showing the relative ages of groups and corresponding profiles along the perimeters. The diameters of the groups are one-and-a-half times the height of the mature trees

Although more commonly regarded as a system particularly suited to broad-leaved forest, the Group Selection System can be applied with equal success to mixtures. Within limits dictated by the species and especially by their windfirmness, it can also be applied to pure conifer forest.

The Group Selection Forest. The adoption of this system results in the creation of a forest complex which, once established, will never change overall. Individual parts will go through the familiar stages of young crop, saplings, young and older saplings, and large trees; but the forest as a whole will remain essentially the same, all the constituents being constant in the proportion of ground that they occupy.

With the limited size of group envisaged, at any one point the full range of size-classes will be visible, producing the effect so highly desirable both from the conservation and amenity points of view — open glades among stately trees of all sizes. At the same time it will be possible at any stage to initiate changes in the species used and in any mixtures employed; and by judicious manipulation, to retain fine specimens to considerable age, to create vistas, to preserve screens, maintain a forest canopy where erosion is threatened, and to preserve important ecosystems.

CHAPTER 8

Conversion to Group Selection of Even-Aged Woods

Conversion to group selection of even-aged woods is fairly straightforward, involving the cutting of groups and re-stocking at the rate determined by the choice of rotation-age and felling-cycle. The distribution of the groups can, in this case, be formalized in planning by the use of squared paper to ensure that, wherever possible, new fellings are not made until the adjoining growth is at least tall enough to provide side-shade to the new plants or seedlings. The actual phasing of the conversion will depend on the age of the crop when this is initiated.

An example of this type of formalized conversion is provided by the treatment of an 80-hectare wood in north Lincolnshire in which some recent felling had shown a high incidence of shake in the old oak trees. The wood stood on almost level land, surrounded by arable fields, and was within a few miles of a large town. Clear-falls of any extent would have resulted in a serious alteration to the overall appearance of the wood. A solution was provided by dividing the whole wood into 1.2-hectare sections, as far as possible rectangular in shape, the length of each being approximately twice the width. The long axis was aligned in a north-south direction so that the maximum amount of sunlight could reach the soil whenever a block was felled for re-stocking. The numbering of the blocks made it possible to arrange that none would be felled until and unless it was sheltered on all sides, either by large trees of the old crop or by newly-stocked areas that had reached the stage at which they were due for their first thinning. This ensured the maximum degree of shelter consonant with the maximum degree of insolation, involving a wide scatter of successive felled and re-stocked blocks. As a result the wood, when seen from outside, appeared to be unaltered in its overall conformation, and it has continued to appear so for over 30 years since the first fellings began. This satisfactory appearance can be expected to continue in perpetuity provided that the same system remains in operation.

Wedge-felling. An alternative method of conversion is by the application of wedge-felling. This method is particularly suitable for use on large landed estates where the woods form an integral and essential part of the appearance of the whole. On such estates there is invariably a strong feeling that the work of such masters as Brown and Repton should not be disturbed.

But woods that are not rejuvenated by natural regeneration or planting will inevitably decay. Treatment is required, to ensure not only that the woods continue to present the same general appearance when viewed from the outside but also that their management is directed to the attainment of growth on a sustained basis. To meet these requirements the Group Selection System has been found to be specially suitable. This provides for the fellings to be spread both in space and in time, limited to comparatively small individual areas. Overall the appearance of the woods does not change.

However, there are some circumstances in which this system in its simplest form is either difficult to apply or is undesirable for other reasons. For example, the woods may be on a steep slope where the downhill extraction of timber may cause damage to re-stocked groups lying below. There may be difficulties also where restricted felling areas are not acceptable and where sizeable areas have to be felled to meet the requirements of potential timber buyers. A large parcel of standing timber will generally be more attractive to buyers than a number of smaller ones spread over a large wood.

These special problems can be overcome in many cases by the adoption of a system of felling in wedges. This is not to be confused with the classical German Wedge System which was developed in the Wurttemburg Black Forest. This system was primarily intended to cope with the danger of windblow in mountain areas and consisted essentially of the progressive removal of the crop by the expansion of narrow wedges. In contradistinction to this, wedge-felling provides for the removal of the trees from an area of woodland in two successive fellings in a series of broad triangles which, on level ground, may be more or less equilateral.

The method is best explained by considering the simple case of a large wood bounding the park of an historic mansion. It is assumed that the shape and appearance of the wood are of great importance, being originally designed by one of the great landscapers as part of the estate layout. It is necessary that there should be a ride, more or less centrally aligned and parallel to the park boundary of the wood. Triangular wedges are felled in such a way that their apices lie on this ride, the bases of the felling areas being on the park boundary.

Extraction to the park is simple and presents no problems. When it is completed, the felled triangles are re-stocked by planting, perhaps with the assistance of some natural regeneration from the standing trees. The appearance of the wood from a distance is now little different from what it was before. There is no break in the line of the tree-tops and the new young growth will soon mask the exposed unfurnished parts of the older trees. Only an observer standing immediately opposite the centre of the base of each triangle will see deep into the wood; from positions to either side the felled and re-stocked areas will be partially obscured to a degree which will depend on the observer's situation relative to the centre-line of each individual wedge. Since the observer can only be on the centre-line of one wedge at any one time, his view of the felled areas will always be a restricted one.

When the trees on the re-stocked wedges have grown to a sufficient height, the wedges initially left standing will then be felled. The period adopted will be half the notional rotation. The section of the wood behind the central ride will be treated in the same way as those facing the park, the felling taking place at the same time. The wedges to be felled in this section will be situated immediately behind the standing wedges facing the park. In this way there will not normally be any weak spots at the meeting of the apices that might betray the presence of felled areas beyond the ride. This is clearly shown in Figure 7.

In practice the size and shape of the triangles can be adapted to suit the terrain. In hilly areas, shape will generally be the prime factor in deciding

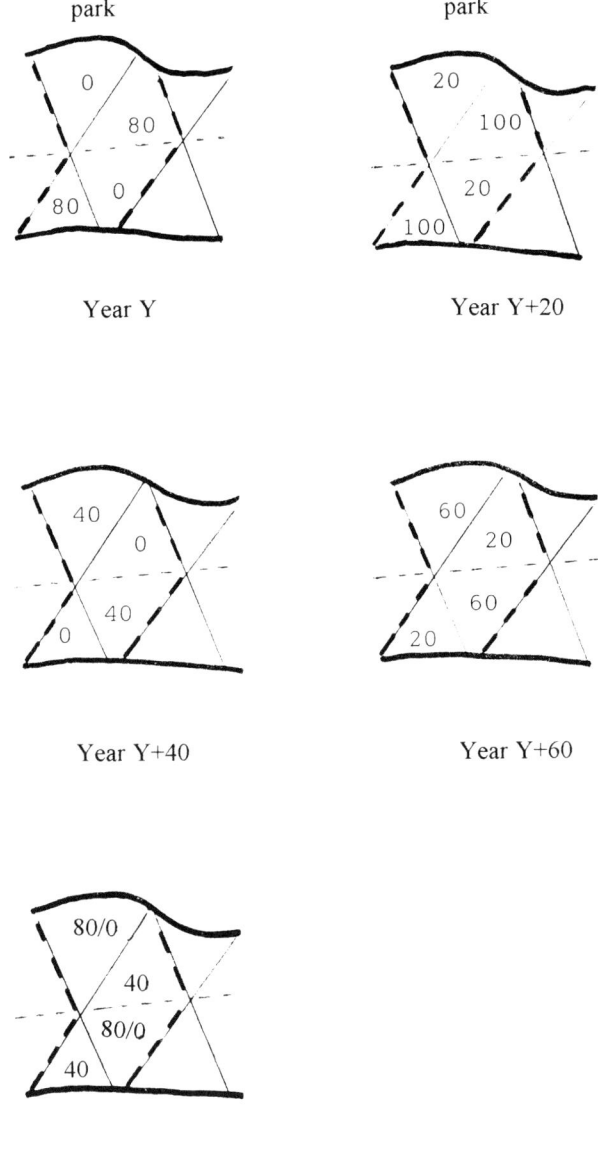

Figure 7. Wedge-felling. Diagram showing a typical layout with the ages of the coupes at intervals of 20 years, assuming that felling begins when the even-aged crop is 80 years old. From the Year+40 (when all the old crop has been felled), the pattern stabilizes

how the system is to be applied. Its employment can be of special value when felling is to take place on tree-covered ridges where exposure of a bare skyline must be avoided for visual reasons. In such cases the centrally-aligned ride will be along the crest of the ridge.

In addition to its importance from the visual amenity aspect, the system provides all the advantages of the Group Selection System, of which it is an extreme example. These consist essentially of flexibility in the use of both light-demanding and shade-bearing species; of shade and shelter with the benefits of edge effect; of simplified extraction; and avoidance of excessive exposure of the soil. In certain conditions the reduced susceptibility to windblow claimed for the German Wedge System may also apply. Additional advantages are those shared with the working of rotational coppice — the provision of conservation corridors and also of shooting stands. The latter are normally difficult to arrange where large clear-fellings are undertaken.

The disadvantages are limited to those shared by all systems involving planting or natural regeneration, lying mainly in the need to control all deer, rabbits and squirrels. Where fencing has to be undertaken, much of the total length required can be of a permanent character since only the bases of the wedges and a short length at the apices will need to be removed to allow timber to be extracted.

An example of the application of the system to a single wood may be quoted from a visually sensitive area of the Cotswold escarpment. The wood consisted of a fully-stocked crop of beech about 120 years old, standing on a very steep slope facing the Vale of Gloucester. A minor public road ran along its upper boundary and a stoned track along the contour forming its lower boundary, below which there was a younger wood. The decision to undertake the initial felling was made when a good mast occurred. The bases of the wedges were marked out along the contour track, the apices being on the upper road. Trees in these wedges were then marked for felling.

Sample quadrats having indicated a weight of beech-mast totalling several tons to the acre (this was before the metric system was introduced), the owner's herd of pedigree pigs was introduced to the wood and confined by a temporary electric fence. Their only other food was an occasional load of windfall cider apples. On this diet the animals fattened very satisfactorily for several months, at the same time treading-in a proportion of the mast and mixing the leaf-mould with the mineral soil.

The pigs were then removed and the marked trees felled. Extraction was downhill to the contour track. The following spring a satisfactory crop of beech seedlings appeared on the felled wedges and also in parts of the wedges left standing, where side light had penetrated. Unstocked gaps were then planted with beech and larch.

Twenty years later the remaining wedges were felled and the resulting bare areas planted as necessary to supplement the natural regeneration. From one of the main roads crossing the Cotswold escarpment, only one mile distant, the visual effect of the fellings was negligible and only local residents, and riders and walkers along the contour track (part of the Cotswold Way), appeared to be aware that the whole wood had in fact been felled and re-stocked in two stages.

CHAPTER 9

Conversion to Group Selection of Unmanaged Woodland and Scrub

Small woods. Untended and decaying woods are unfortunately still a familiar sight in the countryside of England and Wales. By far the majority are of mainly broad-leaved character and a high proportion belong to farmers. Small areas of woodland provide useful shelter for stock, nesting for an occasional pheasant, and undisturbed cover for rabbits and perhaps a hare. They also add to the appearance of a farm; the countryside looks very bare where there are no small woods to break up the wide stretch of fields. But there is little profit to be derived from them. Clear-felling carries with it, under current law, the obligation to replant and to maintain the resulting crop, burdens that a busy farmer operating with a minimum staff, or none at all, is often unwilling to undertake. In consequence nothing is done to the wood, the trees grow on slowly until an occasional one falls and is cut up for firewood.

Some of these woods are of old coppice that has been neglected and is dying back; some still represent the relics of wartime fellings that have never been taken in hand; others have had the best trees removed over a period of years to raise cash in difficult times; and some have been virtually de-forested, with fences deliberately removed or allowed to collapse to provide winter shelter for stock. How can woods of this sort be brought back into production, to become once again useful and attractive timber-producing assets?

There are a number of ways in which this can be done and it will be convenient to consider first a method advocated by the Ministry of Agriculture. This proposes the clear-felling and replanting of groups and has certain attractions to those farmers whose woods contain saleable timber. Selected patches are felled and replanted with metre-high trees protected individually with plastic sleeves or tree-shelters to avoid the high cost of fencing. The timber felled will generally more than pay for the cost of the work if grants are available; and the farmer may well feel that he has taken a useful and profitable step along the road to forest management. But he has probably chosen some of his best — that is, most valuable — woodland in which to site his groups, which implies that the remainder left standing will be of poorer quality. As group-planting in this way requires the retention of surrounding cover for a considerable period of years, both for shelter and because a too-rapid return to open up more groups would quickly remove the wood from the landscape, the remaining wood will continue to decay for many years. In other words, this kind of felling and replanting of groups does not of itself result in a group selection forest system, which requires not only detailed planning but also continued skilled management. Farm forestry in this country has suffered and will continue to suffer from lack of continuity of care, since the farmer is, in these days of high wages, chronically short of labour at the time of year when it is urgently needed for weeding in the woods.

In fact small woods do not lend themselves to the Group Selection System, since the opening of groups extensive enough to provide the right conditions is liable to involve too large a proportion of the area of the wood and to leave an insufficient area standing to make a viable second 'group' at some future date. An alternative in such cases is to convert each individual small wood, in rotation, to a coppice-with-standards condition, as described earlier. The ultimate resort is to convert the woods to coppice, by felling and then protecting the new stool-shoots until they are out of danger from grazing by rabbits and deer, or stock.

Larger woods. Where woodlands are of greater extent, conversion to the Group Selection System is usually possible. Such woods typically consist of a mixture of unthinned trees of all ages and quality, from large-headed over-mature standards to dense thickets of natural regeneration. Most of the woods of this character are broad-leaved and the following prescriptions are based on this assumption.

The first step* is to identify groups of trees that by their quality can be expected to continue to improve if judiciously thinned. The total area of such groups should represent the proportion of broad-leaves that it is desired to maintain as a permanent constituent of the wood. This may vary in individual cases from, perhaps, one third where financial returns are important, to the whole area of the wood where only amenity considerations are taken into account. In the latter case all planting would be with broad-leaves, except where conifer nurses were required. Where a proportion only is to be maintained as permanent broad-leaved high forest, the first step will be to clear-fell all except the selected groups and to replant with groups of fast-growing conifers. Each group may be of one species only or of a mixture, and the groups will be of approximately even size, comparable to that of the selected broad-leaved groups.

All crops will be given the normal treatment according to plantation forestry practice, being thinned at five-year intervals from the age of, say, 15 years. At age 30, one twelfth of the total replanted conifer area will be felled and re-stocked, the fastest-growing areas being chosen. Similar action will be taken every fourth year thereafter. If conversion began in the year A, then by year A+74 the whole conifer area will be operating on a rotation of 44 years, the oldest and finest trees (probably larch of 'boat-skin' quality) having just been felled at the age of 74. The unavoidable length of the first rotation for some groups thus allows the retention of the finest and probably the slower-growing trees to be carried on beyond the age at which felling would normally take place.

The broad-leaves would be treated in a similar manner, felling and re-stocking of the first group taking place in year A+10, with successive fellings of groups comprising one sixth of the total area every tenth year where ash, sycamore, wild cherry, and birch were constituents of the crop being grown on a 60-year rotation. Where oak or beech is grown on a rotation of 120 years, the area felled and re-stocked every tenth year would be one twelfth of the total area of the original groups. In this way a series of ten-year age-classes up to 60 years and 120 years would be established by years A+70 and A+130 respectively.

---

* The method outlined would be unlikely to meet the current (1994) requirements of the British Forest Authority. Its acceptance is more probable at some later date when the Group Selection System is more widely practised.

Conversion from scrub. One of the greatest challenges facing a manager is how to convert woodland that has been divested of its best timber, and then neglected, into a productive state at the least cost and with the least loss of time. At the end of the Second World War it was estimated that over 40 per cent of the privately-owned woodland in Great Britain was either cleared, derelict, or devastated as a result of the enormous wartime demand for timber in the absence of the normal imports.

The following is an account of the methods adopted on a large Cotswold estate, where the woods concerned totalled about 480 hectares. Prior to the war they had consisted of beech, oak, ash, sycamore and larch, below which there was hazel and, in places, wych-elm (*Ulmus glabra*). Cutting of the coppice on a rotational basis had ceased many years previously. During the war all trees over 40 centimetres at breast-height had been felled, except for avenue trees along the main rides. Little regard was paid to the smaller trees during the felling and extraction, with the result that many were badly damaged. As the underwood was not cut before felling began, a great deal of it was smashed and broken, being left in some places in a tangled mass. In one respect the woods were more fortunate than on some estates since they contained no old tops overgrown with bramble and bracken. A clear agreement with the Ministry of Supply had ensured that this burden was not added.

Casual inspection showed little of value remaining in the woods; but detailed investigation revealed a considerable quantity of young ash with clean butts, though with somewhat restricted crowns. There were also groups of sycamore poles worth helping, though many had been damaged in the crown by grey squirrels. A proportion of the oak remaining looked capable of putting on useful increment. In addition there were groups of established regeneration of sycamore and ash, with a little birch. To set against this, rabbits abounded, the squirrel population was very large in peak years, and fallow deer roamed in the woods.

In deciding on the treatment to be employed, the following considerations had to be borne in mind. First, a productive crop of some sort had to be established cheaply over the whole area in the shortest possible time; once this had been done, it would be comparatively simple to improve it later. Secondly, the general broad-leaved character of the woods had to be preserved, while at the same time it was necessary to introduce a rather higher proportion of European larch and Scots pine, for which the woods were noted in the past. And thirdly, cover for game had to be preserved and the overall appearance of the woodland maintained during the conversion period.

Furthermore, experience gained in another large wood nearby that had been clear-felled showed how inadvisable it was to undertake widespread clearing. In this wood forest conditions had been lost even up to eight years after felling and, with the surface soil dried out by wind and sun, the re-establishment of tree-growth remained severely checked.

These considerations, coupled with the fact that the fellings had not been sufficiently heavy to cause any major disturbance of the forest climate or soil, emphasized the importance of enlisting the aid of all possible natural seedling growth and coppice, and of reducing clearing for planting to a minimum. As much of the advance growth was in groups, the group was adopted as the working basis. In addition to groups of advance growth, any trees that were retained were if possible to be kept in groups. Plantings, too, were to be in pure (single species) groups, approximating in size to the natural ones and set between them. Thus a form of group selection was to be established right from the start, and the need for future clear-fellings avoided. Rabbits had to be drastically reduced and three keepers were given the prime task of destroying them over the 480-hectare block of woodland.

In practice, three techniques or treatments were developed.

1. Where stocking with trees, poles, and seedlings was complete:
A great deal of heavy work was required to bring such areas into a productive state, as the material present was in an extremely raw condition. Typically it consisted mainly of widely-spaced and rather small oak, sycamore, and ash, many being of poor shape with poor crowns and mostly damaged during the felling operations. Below and around them were patches of advance growth of sycamore, ash, and birch, some small and badly nibbled by rabbits, some large, whippy and bent, with a tangle of brambles to a height of 1.5 metres around their stems. Other ash seedlings were found emerging from dense patches of bramble. And scattered throughout, obstructing the growth of seedlings everywhere, was old broken hazel coppice. In their untreated state such

areas were virtually impassable in summer except along old dragging-tracks. The prescriptions were as follows:

a. Cut all hazel and other underwood.

b. Thin out groups of advance-growth to about 0.75 metre spacing, retaining the best stems, and cutting the others cleanly back to the ground. The latter would shoot again and might be of some use later. Keep spacing close, as stems of this kind, grown in dense clumps, were often very thin and whippy, and unable to stand alone if opened too much at first.

c. Reduce to one shoot per stool any useful ash or sycamore coppice-poles. Poles to be retained should be of good shape and break from a point low down on the stool so that, as they grew in girth, they might put out new roots of their own and not be forced to depend on the old roots of the partially-decayed stool.

d. Fell all trees in the overwood that either had no prospect of putting on useful increment or were not required as seed-bearers or to provide shelter. Where the overwood was thick there would be a wide choice and shelter would be provided by vigorous trees of good shape. Where the overwood was thin, some rather inferior trees might have to be kept for a while.

The felling was of some delicacy and not normally to be entrusted to a timber merchant. The direction of fall of each tree had to be decided with reference to the surrounding mass of natural regeneration and to the line of extraction that it could most conveniently share with others. Cording of the tops and burning of brush had to be done before the timber was removed. This was done preferably with a rear-winch tractor, the butts being hauled in a straight line to the nearest arterial dragging-track and thence to a convenient ride for loading. When timber extraction was completed, the same routes were used for the extraction of the cord-wood. In this way comparatively little damage was done. When falling crowns unavoidably destroyed advance-growth, this was cut back to shoot again clean. The dragging-tracks themselves, which were often worn deep with the surface-soil torn off and the clay puddled and compacted, might remain uncolonized by new seedlings for many years. As, however, extraction routes were always required under this system, firstly for bean-sticks from early thinnings and later for larger material, this was no disadvantage, provided that the original layout was correct.

2. *Where stocking with trees, poles, and seedlings was incomplete. Full treatment:*

Such areas were similar in many ways to those described above, but contained considerable blanks where no utilizable tree-growth was to be found. Typically their openness led to a strong coppice-growth, with heavy bracken or bramble. The few larger trees in these open patches generally occurred singly, rarely in groups. As between seven and ten years had elapsed since the wartime felling, it was reasonable to assume that such areas were unlikely to become colonized in the near future. It was these blank areas that were planted.

Treatment began with the clearing of the weed in the blank areas, and for this an autoscythe was used with considerable success. When sporadic ash or sycamore regeneration occurred among this weed, for instance half-metre ash under heavy bracken, its presence was ignored and the whole mown off together, the young trees being cut as low to the ground as possible. Following the cutting and burning-up of the weed, operations continued along the lines indicated for Treatment 1 above. After extraction of all timber and firewood had been completed, the whole area, or that part of it containing substantial blanks, was wired in with a rabbit-fence.

Planting then proceeded in the blanks between the groups of regeneration. Details of the technique varied, but generally the plants were massed in pure groups about 20 metres in diameter, this being comparable with the average size of a natural group of ash or sycamore. In cases where the blanks were of considerable size, the planted groups were arranged in chequerboard fashion. As indicated previously, European larch and Scots pine were used a great deal in this work; but more variety was considered desirable and other species were also introduced, though on a much smaller scale. Shade-bearers are of special value in work of this kind and it was expected that western hemlock (*Tsuga heterophylla*) might play an important part in later developments. At the corners of these large groups, small groups of beech were inserted, employing nine plants as against the 144 of the conifer groups, with the intention of producing one tree from each group without a superabundance of worthless thinnings. Only beech from the estate's own prime stock was used. Planting was at an orthodox spacing of 1.5 metres except where sporadic regeneration existed. Since one natural seedling between two plants would reduce the effective spacing by half, in such locations the spacing was increased to three metres. Plants were set out in straight lines in the ordinary way for convenience in planting and early weedings, the groups of advance growth being 'leap-frogged' and the lines being continued beyond. No beating-up was considered necessary in these areas owing to the constant supply of new seed from the seed-bearers.

3. Where stocking with trees, poles, and seedlings was incomplete. Partial treatment in advance:
This consisted simply in the cutting of the old hazel in compartments not scheduled for very early treatment but in which acceptable natural regeneration had appeared. These big hazel stools threw a great deal of shade, thus preserving a clean floor below. This was often found to be sown densely with ash or sycamore seedlings, one or two years old. If left unassisted the majority of these would die from lack of light or at best straggle out towards light gaps as bent and partially-suppressed stems of no value. If freed by the cutting of the hazel, they were able to grow rapidly into straight-stemmed groups of advance-growth, ideal material among which to carry out the method of conversion first described. Many hazel-stools did indeed shoot again although a high proportion were too old and weak to recover; but the space occupied by their young shoots was only a fraction of the original area covered. No other steps were taken at this stage beyond the cutting of the coppice and burning of the brush. The whole object of the operation was to give the area a chance to improve its condition before it became due for intensive treatment.

It will be observed that only Treatment 2 above provides for the introduction of conifers or other broad-leaved species not already present. This aspect of the rehabilitation was deliberately subordinated to the necessity for getting the whole area of the woodland under productive crops in the shortest possible time. It was expected that oak and beech would spread gradually into areas of ash where the light available would be sufficient for young seedlings. They would have priority when cleanings and early thinnings took place in the regeneration groups, resulting in an increase in their numbers over the years. It was also planned in due course to plant beech and larch in gaps resulting from subsequent fellings of mature trees from time to time, and in suitable areas to create gaps artificially for this purpose.

CHAPTER 10

Control of the Felling in Irregular Woods

The silvicultural management of woodlands has been discussed earlier. The division of the woods into compartments for working is based on detailed information concerning the existing crop of trees and the site on which it is growing — its geology, drainage, aspect and exposure. This information forms the basis of any plan of operations for the working of a woodland area. The decisions arising out of these aspects of the planning offer few problems. What does constitute a difficulty in irregular woodlands is how to ensure that the amount of timber removed over a period of years does not exceed the amount actually grown during that period. It will be seen that the effect of removing more wood than has actually been grown will eventually result in the disappearance of all the large trees. Conversely, if the amount removed during the period has been much less than that produced, the woodland will eventually contain too many old trees and too few young ones. In other words, the stocking of the wood will be out of balance.

In ordinary plantation forestry, as practised in Britain, control of the felling is normally by area; a 'normal' forest would consist of perhaps 80 compartments of equal area, of ages from one to 80 years, one compartment being felled and replanted each year in perpetuity. Since the age-classes in irregular forestry are not distributed by area, some other system of control has to be adopted; and methods currently in use on the

Continent of Europe rely on periodic measurements of the trees.

Conditions in British irregular woods differ considerably from those on the Continent of Europe as typified by Switzerland. In the first place few of these woods are publicly owned, the majority being in private hands. From this follows the second difference in that the staff and facilities are not available for making the necessary inventories and calculations. For this reason the only operation of the Swiss method in Britain has been by, or with the assistance of, university departments of forestry employing student labour. Few private estates of any extent could contemplate the volume of work involved, especially at current labour rates, without such assistance.

As a consequence of this, the impression has arisen that irregular forestry is too difficult and, not being visibly under 'control', is therefore uncontrolled. This is unfortunate, and it arises out of an over-orthodox attitude, as can be seen by examining the question of yield control a little more closely. Yield control, or regulation of the yield, is a device based on the concepts of the normal forest and sustained yield: a forest that goes on for ever, producing the same amount of timber every year. This is the aim of any large-scale forest enterprise since it is the most efficient form of management in terms of labour, supervision and markets. But, in Britain at least, it is only an aim. With very few exceptions indeed, no private woodlands are in a 'normal' state, and none of the state forests are. Why then, if plantation forestry is not 'normal', should it be essential for irregular woodlands to meet this ideal? It is contended here that it will be sufficient if comparable progress is made towards that goal.

If we adopt this more relaxed attitude it is possible to dispense with the heavy burden of successive or continuous inventories. This can be done by making simple ocular estimates of the growing stock, ensuring that there are sufficient numbers of the smaller sizes of trees to provide the correct stocking of large (exploitable) trees in due course.

In theory it would be possible in perfect conditions to operate an irregular forest on the basis of equal numbers of trees in each size-class, one seedling growing into one sapling, growing into one medium-sized tree, growing into one mature tree. Swiss foresters, working on a strict money-yield basis, tend to strive always for refinements in the direction of this ideal; but in Britain, where irregular woodlands are often managed partly at least with amenity considerations in mind, the control of the yield rather than its maximizing, is likely to be the more important aim.

Workers in this field have shown that, by employing figures derived from even-aged plantations, it is possible to calculate for any species the normal number of trees of each size-class that any given wood should contain. The size-classes for this purpose are defined by height rather than by girth or diameter. The number in each class can, moreover, be defined in terms of the number in the largest class. Thus figures derived from the Forestry Commission's tables for sycamore and ash show that in an area of irregular woodland under informed management there should be one-and-one-third times as many trees averaging 24 metres in height as there are with an average height of 26 metres (the largest class); two-and-one-third times as many averaging 16 metres; and 15 times as many averaging nine metres. Thus if there are 120 trees in the largest class, there should be 160 in the next class, 280 in the class below, and 1800 in the youngest or regeneration class.

A succession of checks throughout the wood will show whether the correct distribution of the size-classes is present. And that is all that is necessary to ensure that the wood is in healthy balance.

However, it is possible that the wood may be in balance but not fully productive. This will be the case if the number of trees in the tallest class is less than the figure shown in the tables. A number of small temporary sample plots will be sufficient to show the position. If the mature trees are deficient in number, there may still be sufficient of the smaller classes. This will clearly be shown by the proportional checks made.

A similar series of proportions can be calculated very simply for each species and yield-class; or, in the case of mixtures, of any combination of these. It should be noted, however, that the identification of the classes by height becomes more difficult in broad-leaved trees grown on long rotations. This is seen in beech yield class 10 where the figures, after necessary adjustment, show 110 mature trees per hectare with a height of 34 metres corresponding to an age-class of 101-120, while the next class contains 165 trees with a mean height of 32 metres. Since mature beech have rounded crowns, the difference between 32 and 34 metres will not be easily distinguishable; and the same applies to most other broad-leaved trees. It is probable that in such cases it will be necessary for practical purposes to count the two largest classes together, making an arbitrary division based on observed diameters. Alternatively, a modified system could be adopted, using only three size-class groups — zero to one-third, one-third to two-thirds, and two-thirds to maximum height.

The essential questions to be asked are: first, is the number of mature trees correct or nearly so, and secondly, are there sufficient trees in each of the lower classes to produce this number of mature trees in the future? Provided that ocular checks show that these requirements are satisfied, the wood will be 'normal' and in healthy equilibrium. All that is then required is the application of intelligent thinning of the intermediate classes and informed handling of the marking of the exploitable trees at each cyclical felling.

If ocular checks show that the size classes are not present in the correct proportions, the marking of exploitable trees and of thinnings in the smaller sizes will take the discrepancies into account. It will be unlikely that recovery to normal stocking can be attained in one cycle; a gradual building up of the deficient classes will obviously take time. In this respect the creation of a normal irregular forest does not differ in essentials from the creation of a normal plantation forest.

CHAPTER 11
Avoiding Clear-Felling in Ornamental Plantings

Since the time when a wealthy Englishman's home ceased to be literally a castle, large country houses have almost invariably been associated with trees, generally in groups, avenues or belts, providing shelter and privacy, and a foil to the often austere lines of the buildings themselves.

A very high proportion of these houses date from the period beginning in Queen Anne's reign and ending with accession of Queen Victoria. Fortunately for us today, building became fashionable when the skill, the taste, and the materials were all available. And together with building went the planting of trees. 'Who plants like Bathurst or who builds like Boyle?' was the rhetorical question posed by that witty and keen observer, Pope. The trees provided the only setting worthy of the great piles that arose on gentlemen's estates throughout the country. The trees that our forefathers planted with such foresight, like the houses that they built, are now too often showing signs of their age. For us, in our generation, the problems are those of preservation and restoration.

In the case of houses, the problem is often a clear-cut one. The needs of the building can be ascertained and stated with exactitude by the architect. No challenge in restoration is beyond his skill, and the techniques are available to the modern craftsman, provided only that the necessary funds are available. But the trees …?

Our Georgian forebears were satisfied with the saplings that they planted. Few lived into their nineties like the first Earl Bathurst, who was able to see the trees he had planted grown to full stature. We, on the other hand, have only known the same trees at the end of their lives. To us the setting of the great country houses is one of magnificent beeches, oaks, and limes. When such trees are cut down or have already gone and young trees are planted, we feel a great sense of loss. In fact we appreciate the big house in its setting; without that setting it would be a different and less satisfying thing.

How then are we to preserve the setting? We cannot, as governments now do, make our plans retrospectively. Unless action has already been taken, all we can do is to plan intelligently — now. The commonest method in restoring groves and avenues is to plant young trees where the old ones have already gone, or to create gaps for this purpose by felling the more decrepit of the survivors. Unfortunately this course has several disadvantages. Because the small trees are far over-topped by their big neighbours, they are often deprived of direct light, and are either completely suppressed or they stretch out towards the light and develop a leaning habit. Secondly, it is rarely possible to plant sufficient trees in such a situation to replace the old ones effectively without removing a disproportionate number of the latter. Thus fully to replace a clump or grove, it is not sufficient to plant only half as many trees as it originally contained; while if more than half of the old ones are removed, the character will be lost. And thirdly, the small trees are very vulnerable to damage from branches falling from their moribund neighbours. It can be disastrous when a promising tree, planted perhaps 20 years previously and now actively contributing to the beauty of the clump, is ruined in this way.

A less usual method that is sometimes acceptable is the planting of 'shadow trees' behind the old ones, so placed that when the latter are removed in due course, the new trees will appear to stand almost exactly in their place. This can only be applied when the tree or group of trees is to be seen from one direction. For instance, a park clump as seen from the entrance front of a big house can be 'replaced' in this way. If the clump is viewed from another part of the grounds the replacement planting will be seen to be in a different position. In the treatment of avenues, the corresponding action is to plant a completely new line of trees either inside or outside the original avenue. As the overall appearance is altered, this is not always an acceptable solution.

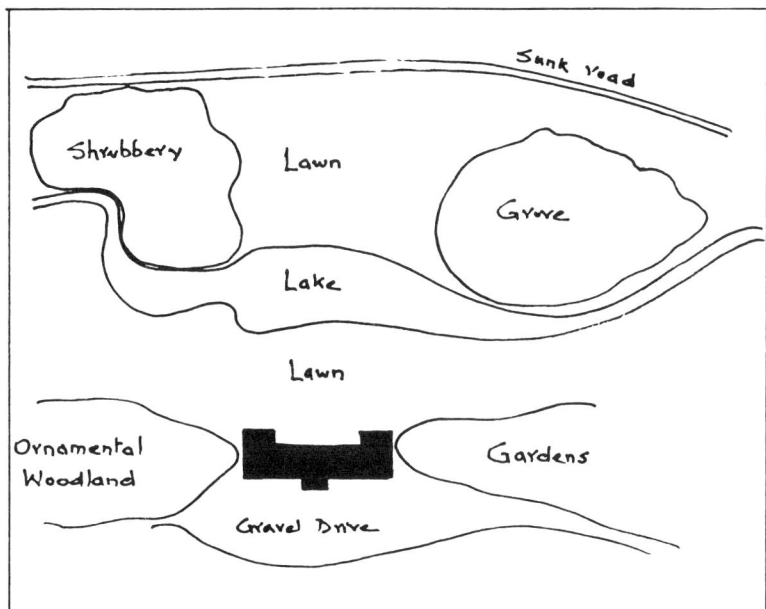

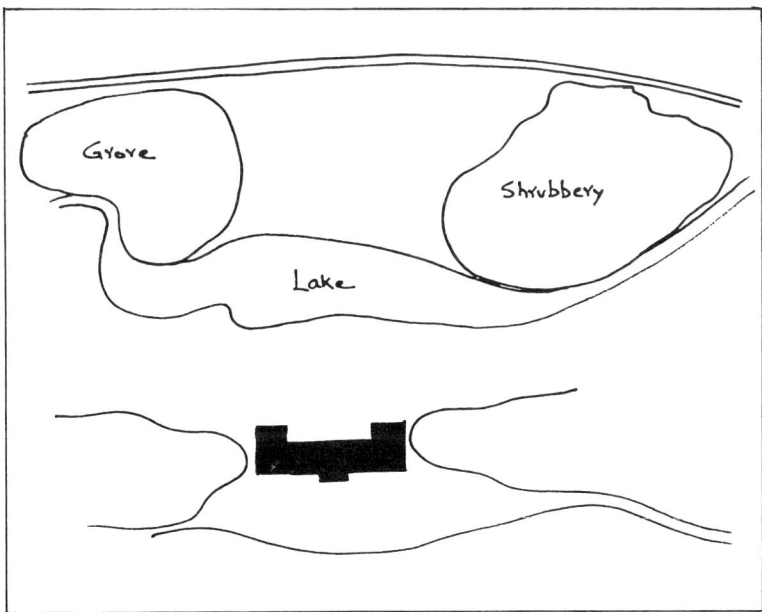

Figure 8. An example of the 'looking-glass' method in the setting of a country house.

A third course is now suggested which is of a more fundamental nature and which contrives to avoid some of the more objectionable features of the methods so far described. This may be called the 'looking-glass' method, not from any connection with Alice but because it aims to create a reversed facsimile of the existing layout. It can be most easily explained by considering an actual problem. Figure 8 shows the relative positions of a country house and three important features in its setting — the lake and a grove of very fine trees which is separated from extensive beds of flowering shrubs by a wide sweep of lawn. The grove is contemporary with the house. The vast oriental plane (*Platanus orientalis*) and massive walnut (*Juglans regia*) are still things of great beauty, while the big beeches that complete the group have many years of life left provided that they are spared by the wind. The trees are too big for inter-planting, which would produce but a feeble replacement when they at last succumbed. A road behind prevents the use of the shadow method, which would be unsatisfactory in any case because the grove is near to the house and distances in relation to the lake are important. The 'looking-glass' method, as can be seen from the diagram, provides for the planting and bringing-on of young trees under cover of the shrub-beds to the pattern actually existing in the grove. If the latter has, say, 40 years more of effective life, the young trees will have developed shape and grace by the time the old trees finally disappear. It will then be possible, with no great disturbance of the layout, to move the shrubs to the site lately occupied by the old trees. The former shrub-beds would then be grassed down around the new grove of well-established trees. To the observer standing on the terrace, the view would be substantially the same as that seen by the owner of the house some 40 years after the original building and planting, but in reverse.

The same principles can be applied to avenues, except where these are aligned between the house and a special feature, such as a monument. Even then, the importance of the layout may warrant the planting of a new avenue, and the removal of the feature to a new site; or, where this is not practicable, the provision of an alternative one.

Groves or clumps in parkland can be treated in several ways. The shadow method is not always acceptable in such situations, as the growing shadow spoils the clean appearance of the park; part of the latter's charm lies in the sharp contrast of the clump against the grazed grassland. Where the clump is viewed principally from the immediate neighbourhood of the house, it can be halved in such a way that the standing half continues to be seen from the house, the new planting on the felled section being hidden. In due course when the young trees reach an acceptably large size, the remainder of the old clump can be felled and replanted in its turn. This system can be employed whether the clump is round, square, or rectangular in shape. Another method, suitable only for the larger clumps, is to remove all but the outermost ring of trees and to replant in the centre. There are two requirements here. One is that there should be sufficient remaining trees to preserve the solid appearance of the clump; the other is that the area for replanting should be sufficiently large to allow adequate light to reach the young trees and to continue to do so for some 30 to 40 years, until they are large enough to be opened up to the view. At this stage the remaining old trees are felled. It is then open to the owner to accept the new clump as a smaller version of its predecessor or to replant the outer ring.

Mature woods standing near the buildings may be large enough for conversion to an irregular structure, and this method also lends itself to the handling of amenity belts and screens, provided that they are of sufficient width. An example may be given of a wood of very high amenity value, its boundary on one side being only some 50 yards from the stable-block of a large house in North Yorkshire. A public road leading to the gates of the house formed the curving boundary along two sides of its roughly square shape. The method adopted was to fell approximately one third of its area in wedges. This allowed felling and extraction of the timber to take place without damaging the trees left standing; it provided sufficient space and light for planting and natural regeneration of the felled wedges; and it left the remaining trees also standing in rough wedges, so that when the time came for further fellings, they too could be carried out without damage either to the tall trees or to the young ones. Within a space of 20 years from the original felling, the wood had become a most attractive mixture of tall mature beech, ash, oak and Scots pine, with a flourishing element of natural and planted beech up to five metres in height.

Amenity belts of adequate size have been treated in a somewhat similar manner by felling groups. The diameter of these groups must be at least one-and-a-half times the height of the surrounding trees to ensure that the young planted trees will have adequate light. If one or two groups of this size are felled at intervals of 15 or 20 years a loose form of group selection will develop, and there will never be any need to clear-fell such belts.

Screening plantings on park boundaries can be handled by either of these two methods. By careful arrangement of the sections to be felled and replanted it is usually possible to avoid any serious deviation from the plans of the original planters. The writer remembers visiting an estate where plantings made by Capability Brown were so revered that no action to restore them could be contemplated by those responsible for their management. It was only shortly after this visit that nature took the decision out of their hands when a winter gale effectively destroyed them. Suitable action 30 or 40 years earlier could have ensured that the setting of that house could have remained virtually unaltered.

Avenues are a special case and a constant source of worry to their owners. Piecemeal replacement of old giants as they deteriorate has been proved to be no satisfactory solution. This was attempted on the Broad Walk in Christ Church Meadows at Oxford. The resulting line of trees could hardly be described as an avenue but the college authorities could not bring themselves to fell the remaining old trees and replant. The unsightly straggle was only satisfactorily removed by the incidence of Dutch elm disease.

Generally, the most satisfactory solution to decaying avenues has been to plant a new avenue parallel to the old one, where this is acceptable; or to take the bull by the horns and fell and replant. However, where the avenue consists of two rows of trees on each side of the road or walk, there is another possible solution. This is to fell the two inner rows, that is the rows immediately on each side of the centre track. This achieves two things; it removes the danger of branches from the decaying trees falling on traffic or on people using the track, and it provides space for the planting of a row of new trees on either side of the track. The trees left will have crowns that are larger on the outer, more exposed side since they have grown in close competition with those now felled. Thus the new trees will not be over-shaded by their branches. And if any of the remaining trees should fall, or shed branches, before the time comes to fell them in their turn, the fall will be outwards where the weight of the crown is greatest, and away from the newly-planted trees. Other solutions that have been adopted, involving the removal of complete sections of the avenue at regular intervals, followed by replanting, do not provide a satisfactory answer, as they meet the requirements of neither appearance nor safety.

Shelter-belts. The restoration or replacement of old shelter-belts poses a comparatively simple problem, especially if additional land alongside is available for planting. As the value of shelter is greatest in the most exposed areas, the belts are often to be seen as prominent features on the skyline. For this reason it is rarely satisfactory to fell half the belt along its length and replant. Owing to the general narrowness of such belts this can result in an unacceptably transparent appearance as well as involving a serious liability to windblow of the newly-exposed trees left standing. The ideal solution is to plant a new belt of more or less equal width along the leeward side of the old belt and separated from it by a ride. This should be wide enough to ensure that the new planting does not stand below the crowns of the old trees. When the new belt has grown to an acceptable height, but not high enough to be liable to windblow, the old belt can be felled and replanted in its turn. Other more radical solutions exist, of course, dependent on the terrain and the individual requirements of the owner. Most of the shelter-belts that are mature or nearing maturity are probably of considerable age, and their planting was planned at a time when systems of agriculture differed from those in operation today. It may be, therefore, that the planting of entirely new belts sited in quite different locations may be more acceptable that replanting the old ones. In such circumstances planting can be planned to meet the current needs, and the old belts felled as soon as the new ones begin to fill their required purpose of providing shelter for stock and buildings. In almost all cases, high-standing belts are of great value, not only to the owner of the property but to the local inhabitants in general. Their correct handling, therefore, is of the greatest importance. Nothing changes the appearance of the downlands of England more than the presence or absence of these high-standing belts, as can be appreciated in those few parts of the Cotswolds in which none are to be seen.

Park plantings of individual trees present special problems. Where a high proportion of the trees aged 200 years or more have gone, their original layout can be ascertained very easily from the old 25-inch Ordnance Survey sheets produced towards the end of last century and generally to be found preserved in cabinets in estate offices. On these editions the individual trees were marked in parkland surrounding large country houses. The planting was often very dense in places, the trees forming sizeable groves; and with modern costs it is rarely feasible to follow the original layout with meticulous accuracy. However, the general plan can be followed, creating clumps or setting out trees at wider spacing than the originals, so that the overall result will be very similar to that intended by the creators of the park.

One of the most important matters to be considered in this type of work is the maintenance of clear lines of sight; that is, the distribution of clumps and individual trees in such a way as to present the appearance of a continuous avenue or to emphasize a landmark of some distinction. Conversely, lines of sight should be established to hide or disguise undesirable developments such as modern farm-buildings or stretches of road carrying heavy traffic.

To sum up, the principal aim when handling old woods or old park plantings should be to ascertain as clearly as possible the intentions of the original planters. These should then be put into effect without slavish regard for what went before but with the object of achieving, in modern terms, the same results.

CHAPTER 12

Re-Stocking by Natural Means

With constantly rising costs and high rates of interest, the attention of managers is inevitably focused increasingly on cheaper methods of establishing crops of trees and re-stocking felled areas. Effort has generally been concentrated on spacing of plants, early returns from thinnings, inter-planting with Christmas trees, and similar devices. All have involved weeding in the early years of the plantation's life and generally some degree of expensive protection as well.

Where second-rotation crops are concerned the advantages of natural regeneration immediately come to mind; and are only too often dismissed almost as quickly for a number of reasons. The most obvious of these are seed-year frequency, the uncertainty of successful germination, and the protection of seedling growth during subsequent felling operations. In the event, some planting is usually found to be necessary.

The advantages of natural regeneration are nevertheless very great where conditions for its adoption are suitable. In forestry practice in France where in the past time has not been an overriding consideration, it is interesting to see how vital has been the adoption of natural regeneration systems, allowing long regeneration periods of up to 40 years. Prior to the modern use of machines to scarify the forest floor in the preparation of a seed-bed, all that was required in these systems was critically-timed manipulation of the canopy with the classical succession of preliminary fellings, seeding fellings, and final fellings. Where early cleanings in the regeneration were done by local peasants cutting faggot-wood under well-established rules, there was little or no expense involved beyond the normal salaries of the professional staff.

The 300-year rotations that produced the magnificent oaks of Tronçais and Bellême can also be related to the same factors. If the trees could be established at no cost, the accountancy was simplified and compound interest could be ignored. When this is considered together with the great devotion, experience and expertise of the French foresters, it is no surprise to find such magnificent forests in that country. At the same time, the happy result of these controlling factors does suggest some questions concerning our own forestry in Britain.

Unlike the French, we do not enjoy a surplus of land and have never done so throughout many hundreds of years. At present there is a greater pressure than there has ever been on our limited area, since the importance of conservation and rural access for the town-dweller have become generally recognized. Neither do we enjoy all the advantages of the freedom that a long time-scale can provide. The fact that Britain has a smaller proportion of forest land than almost any other country in Europe means that the forest estate must be built up, or restored after felling, as quickly as possible. Natural regeneration systems can be employed and a certain amount of use is made of them. But conditions attached to grants for planting are not geared to extended regeneration periods; and unless some more suitable form of incentive and support is devised there is unlikely to be any significant extension of these systems. The shortage of time is therefore critical.

So the only way in which we find ourselves in a similar position to the traditional one of the French forester is that today we have little money. The Forestry Commission grant-schemes vary from year to year and the traditional landowner continues to be taxed at a punitive level.

It is important, however, not to dismiss these considerations without attempting to derive some lessons from them. In a period when land, time and money are short, we may have to adopt unorthodox methods — and indeed this is being done in various directions in the research sphere at the present time.

Suckers. Coppicing has no useful part to play in irregular forestry; but there is another system, somewhat analogous to coppicing, that has definite possibilities for sustained yield forestry; this is the exploitation of the ability of certain species of trees to produce suckers. In this context these may be described as shoots arising from the side-roots of trees and depending on the parent roots for minerals, water and stored food in their early stages of growth; but which become capable of producing their own root-systems and so becoming totally independent at an early stage. Suckers may arise and survive satisfactorily during the life of the mother tree but appear to receive a strong stimulus when the latter is felled. This no doubt reflects the fact that the whole product of stored sugars, water, and minerals from the entire rooting system of the old tree becomes available to the existing suckers. They benefit also from the additional light enjoyed when the overhead shade is removed.

Thus suckers have the advantage of initial vigour and rapid growth when released by the felling of the over-crop. This also stimulates the production of new suckers so that if the pre-existing ones are damaged during felling an additional supply becomes available. There are thus great advantages over seedling regeneration. Again, since suckers may be produced for considerable distances along the lateral roots of the parent trees, incidental gaps in a crop can be filled by this means. In this way it is possible for the whole of a felled area to be fully restored to a productive state.

The dramatic impact of Dutch elm disease has made the suckering ability of the elm familiar to almost everyone. The success of the English elm, although almost invariably infertile, in perpetuating its species around the hedgerows of southern Britain is the greatest testimony to the viability of this method of propagation. In this context it is relevant to refer to the freedom with which the white and grey poplars (*Populus alba* and *P. canescens*) produce suckers, since the latter is one of the species advocated as a replacement for elm in our denuded hedgerows, as it produces mature trees of somewhat similar form. Other species that sucker freely are the native wild cherry, aspen, grey alder (*Alnus incana*), sweet chestnut, some limes, and robinia (*Robinia pseudoacacia*). The range is not great but wild cherry, grey poplar, sweet chestnut and lime can grow to timber trees of large size, and the other species listed also produce useful material for firewood, turnery, and other purposes.

When trees of these species are felled, it is normally only necessary to protect the new growth from grazing for a few years and then thin to the best stems when they reach a height of two to three metres. One or two further thinnings will bring the crop into the pole-stage — with no cost for plants, planting, beating-up, weeding, and probably no brashing cost since the dense crop will tend to clean itself. In this way a useful and attractive crop of trees can be produced at almost no cost. In the case of cherry, chestnut, and lime this means that for a rotation of, say, 80 years there will be very small costs to be compounded at high interest rates.

The wild cherry, which is quick-growing and produces valuable timber, is specially suited to this treatment; it is resistant to squirrel attack, and it suckers freely. In fact, in grass it will produce a mass of suckers within a radius of ten metres in 15 years. Indeed a wood could in theory be established on bare grassland by simply planting 1.2- to 1.5-metre cherries at 18 metres apart, or, say, 30 to the hectare. After some 15 years without any attention one could expect to have 12 15-year old cherries, probably rather squat and branchy, surrounded by a more or less dense crop of straight clean suckers. In due course, these would require thinning out and spacing, while the original rougher trees could either be felled and left lying (since they would have little value) or be retained below the canopy of their suckers as a continuing source of new growth. As anyone should be able to plant 30 trees on a hectare, this could well be regarded as do-it-yourself afforestation, well-suited to the planting-up of small areas of waste ground.

When contemplating the re-stocking of a felled area there would appear to be a good deal to be said for considering a crop that will replace itself in due course by suckers. And for hedgerow tree planting the advantages are too obvious to be ignored.

Colonization. The absence of vermin is one key to the economical establishment of woodland. A Scottish landowner once told the writer that whenever he was short of money for his forestry enterprise, he used to plant a further area on his moorland property. With light heather, and no rabbits or sheep, he had found that he could plant for less than the planting grant, and have a balance in hand. And indeed, in similar circumstances the easiest method of establishing woodland is by simple neglect. A continuing example is seen in the New Forest, where open areas are only maintained in that condition by the deliberate destruction of seedling growth of Scots pine and birch by intensive grazing or artificial means. A similar situation would develop in many parts of the West Highlands of Scotland if the sheep were removed or fenced out. An example is provided by the building of a new bungalow at the head of one of the famous sea lochs. The surrounding few acres were fenced against sheep, and within a matter of two or three years young pine trees were appearing in such numbers as to constitute a nuisance.

CHAPTER 13
Planting: some Basic Considerations

In describing the Group Selection System it was mentioned that, in addition to natural regeneration, there would generally be a need for some planting. In many cases the planting would probably in fact constitute the greater element in the re-stocking of the gaps created by the group fellings. Not only is it needed where no regeneration occurs, but also where a superior provenance of the same species is required or where completely different species are to be introduced into the forest.

Each group under this system becomes a small even-aged crop on its own and is subject to most of the considerations that apply to large-scale planting. It is appropriate at this point, therefore, to consider these, and in doing so to look into some of the basic factors involved.

Woods consist axiomatically of a large number of individual trees and it is essential to consider the individual as well as the composite whole. In the past, British foresters have tended to operate in a small and somewhat blinkered environment where the tending of trees was concerned. It is only in comparatively recent years that they have looked out to see what other cultivators of trees have been doing. This has no doubt been partly a result of the way that effort has been concentrated on the cultivation of conifers following the formation of the Forestry Commission whose express duty was the production of a reserve of timber to meet the nation's need in time of war. This implied the provision of home-grown substitutes for the vast amount of timber that had to be imported during two world wars. The requirement was for softwood timber, produced by the pines and spruces, which accounts for some 90 per cent of all the timber used in Britain.

So the broad-leaved trees really only came under serious review in the 1970s and 80s. But even then there was, and still appears to be, a tendency to initiate research projects without first finding out what other operators had already discovered. The volume of information available from centuries of concentrated work with fruit trees was not made use of. The lessons learnt from the growing of apples and pears remain a closed book to most foresters. The individual tree has too long been ignored by those responsible for whole forests.

Variety and provenance. All apples are derived originally from the crab (*Pyrus malus*) but among cider-apples alone there were between 100 and 200 separate and quite distinct varieties in common cultivation until quite recently. How many varieties of English oak (*Quercus robur*) are actually distinguished? Or how many of the common beech? A double handful of each, perhaps, and these only recognized by the appearance of their leaves — not for their useful qualities as in the case of apples. Yet both these well-known and much-used forest trees have been grown and planted in Britain for hundreds of years.

Regional variation among Britain's broad-leaved trees is recognized by foresters who work closely with them. Beech on the Cotswolds will differ from Chiltern beech; ash in the Pennines may have quite different characteristic from ash in, say, South Wales, and sycamore in East Anglia may have a bark character entirely different from sycamore in parts of Yorkshire. Indeed, this local variation in sycamore provides perhaps the strongest evidence to suggest that its introduction may have taken place in Roman rather than Elizabethan times.

The local variants are sometimes called 'races', implying a closer definition than the wider 'provenance'. Their very existence indicates a local development attuned to the geology, soil, and climate of their region. They are the natural trees of that region, and the local race is thus the one that will best thrive there. The local race, provided that it will not only grow well but also produce good timber, is the one to be grown and perpetuated.

Race therefore is of first importance in selecting seed for new planting.

It is equally of importance where re-stocking is intended to be by natural means since the presence of seed-bearers of an unsatisfactory race will only ensure the perpetuation of an inferior crop of trees. At this stage it is essential to determine whether the seed-bearers are actually of poor race or whether their poor quality is due to early mismanagement or other reasons, as mentioned earlier.

The two greatest liabilities to which oak is prone are shake and epicormic branching. Although neither has been definitively explained so far, the indications are that the liability to each of these conditions is largely inherited. Certainly in the case of epicormic branching one can see in almost every wood individual oak trees quite free of epicormics while all around the neighbouring trees show strong growth of these adventitious shoots, although the site and light conditions are in every way identical. These may well prove to be inherited characteristics.

In general, provided that the local race of tree can be identified and is known to grow satisfactorily, it should be used. Assuming that it has developed in that region since the retreat of the ice at the end of the last ice-age, it will be well adapted to the conditions in which it is to be grown. Importation of trees of a race from another region of Britain may not result in the same degree of success measured in terms of rate of growth, straightness, frost-hardiness and resistance to disease. The importation of stock from Continental European sources is to be avoided. Not only may the dangers to the immediate crop be greater but the whole of the regional stock stands the risk of being degraded by the dilution of its gene-pool.

Quality of plants. Experience indicates that, if the initial fencing is ignored, the cost of the plant and its planting is often less than that of its after-care, in the form of weeding and beating-up failures. It is therefore vitally important to ensure that one has the very best plant and that one plants in the best way. Planting in the wood can rarely be mechanized or cheapened. Concentration must be on buying the best plant — which, in relation to the labour of planting, is comparatively cheap — and in getting it to grow quickly out of danger from frost and weeds. At this stage we are considering planting in a conventional manner at conventional spacings; tube- and shelter-planting will be dealt with later. Plants should be of good provenance, the best available and preferably local-grown, with good root-systems produced by transplanting or under-cutting, and with strong leaders above a well-branched stem. This implies careful grading of the stock when lifted in the nursery. It will pay to get the best plants even if the cost appears high.

Growing of young broad-leaved plants. It is well-known that, although ash seed when naturally ripened takes two years to germinate, the seed if collected and sown when green will germinate in one year. A fact not so well-known is that sycamore of plantable size can also be produced in one year in a favourable season. Natural seedlings in the cotyledon or 'two-strap' stage can be collected easily from any suitable site. This may be on sand, on a sawdust heap, a coke-heap, or anywhere else where abundant germination has taken place on a loose or friable medium. The seedlings are lifted carefully and planted out by dibbling with the finger in well-prepared garden-soil. A worker can do the whole job of lifting and lining-out at the rate of thousands in a day. Given good soil conditions and a good growing season, this method has consistently produced sycamore plants of up to one metre in height in one year on an estate in North Yorkshire where it has been practised for over 30 years. The stimulus to growth may be imparted by the rupturing of the root-hairs or some similar action, and research along these lines might offer a rapid means of producing planting-stock of other species.

Mycorrhiza. This is the term applied to certain fungi that live symbiotically (that is, to the advantage of both) on the roots of green plants, particularly trees and shrubs. They assist the woody plants to absorb nutrients, especially nitrates, from decaying leaf-litter. They may be said to act as highly-specialized additional root-hairs. In an old woodland that has been established for, say, 50 years or more it is probable that there will be a wide distribution of mycorrhiza. Bare-rooted plants, or plants in pots for that matter, will be most unlikely to have this important aid to growth, since they will have been grown from seed in the nursery. Only if the nursery-beds have been inoculated with the appropriate organism can the plants be expected to go into the wood with every advantage. This can of course be assured by dressing the nursery-beds with leaf-litter taken from a wood of the appropriate species — but how often is this done? Natural seedlings growing in the wood are of course inoculated at a very early stage.

Frost. In every case where planting is to take place on bare land, or after felling a crop of trees, it is essential to make an appraisal of the situation with regard to frost. Cold air flows in a similar way to water. It is vital to ensure that it can drain freely off the planting site without being impeded by obstacles on or below it. The presence of walls or thick old hedges across a sloping site will result in a build-up of cold air in winter, producing artificial frost-pockets. If any such obstacles are present it is essential to provide adequate gaps to allow the free flow of cold air, either by dismantling sections of the wall or clearing occasional lengths of the old hedge.

Where frost-tender plants are to be used, it will pay to use plants of between 0.5 and 1.0 metre in height. These will be more expensive; but if the leading bud stands above the frost-layer the tree will grow away immediately from planting, whereas one with its bud below this layer may remain stunted for years. An extreme example of this was seen in East Yorkshire on a step of the escarpment where ash had been planted. There was a large frost-donor area above, in the form of arable fields, and the flow of cold air was impeded by a dense old wood below. Although the ash plants were already about one metre at planting, they grew only one centimetre a year for the first three years because of late spring frosts. In the fourth year there were no spring frosts and the plants put on a full metre of growth in that season.

As frost even on level ground can occur in a layer of cold air lying perhaps 0.6 metres deep, several years of growth can often be saved by using larger plants than normal.

CHAPTER 14
Planting: Systems

The planning of any planting will depend very largely on the site. If it is to follow the felling of an existing crop of trees, this will also be taken into account. In any case the shape and orientation of the new planting should be arranged in such a way as to provide the new crop with all possible initial advantages. It is at this stage that edge-effect should be taken into consideration.

Edge effect. It is a matter of common observation that trees grow more rapidly when planted close to the edge of a standing wood. They appear to be stimulated in some way and to have an advantage over similar trees in the same plantation that are at a distance from the wood. This edge effect may have a considerable bearing on the progress of plantations and of natural regeneration, and it will be of interest to examine it more closely.

Edge effect is most clearly seen where a section of standing woodland has been felled and immediately replanted. After three or four years it will be possible to observe that the plants within, say, ten metres of the standing trees are clearly making better growth than those at, say, 60 metres distance from the wood. Further, the effect can be seen to be greatest close to the standing trees, and to decrease progressively with the distance from them.

It is possible that studies might show a correlation between the height of the standing trees and the distance to which the effect is traceable. The steepness of the curve made by the tops of the young trees seen in section might also be found to be related to the same factor.

The effect is more striking when the felled block is of limited width. Edge effect is now seen on both sides or, if the felled block is enclosed by standing woodland, on all sides. It can be demonstrated that, as the width of the strip decreases, the two edge-effect zones approach one another until a position is reached at which the whole width of the planted strip is enjoying some measure of stimulation. At this stage a cross-section of the plantation has the appearance of a concave meniscus. Further reduction in the width of the planted strip will produce an ultimate state in which the plantation as a whole is receiving the maximum degree of stimulation. This may, in fact, be beyond the point where shading from the standing woodland is exerting an adverse effect. But there will be an optimum width at which maximum stimulation is experienced with minimum interference by shade. This will almost certainly vary with a number of circumstances, among which orientation and degree of insolation are likely to be prominent.

The shape of the familiar 'domes' of regeneration to be seen below gaps in the forest canopy might at first sight appear to contradict these observations. Closer consideration shows, however, that this is not so. In such confined conditions the centre of the dome represents an area of high stimulation by edge effect; the outsides of the dome are so close to the surrounding trees that the edge effect here is more than counterbalanced by the effect of direct shading.

In the extreme case, where gaps are very small, the familiar position is reached at which the trees are said to be 'drawn'.

When trees under the influence of edge effect can be seen to grow perhaps twice as fast, in their early years, as trees not so favourably situated, it becomes a factor that cannot be ignored. For the field forester it suggests methods of bringing plantations rapidly out of check and reducing weeding costs by early and rapid establishment. It provides a rationale for determining the size of group-openings in the canopy for natural regeneration or for group-plantings. It suggests that in these cases the groups should, where possible, be elongated in a north-south direction.

Where a considerable area is to be felled in one block, the advantages of edge effect can be obtained by leaving narrow strips of the old crop at calculated intervals, for later felling, to provide extraction rides. This was done with very satisfactory results on an estate in the north Cotswolds. It was an extreme case, since the crop to be felled was pure hazel coppice of considerable age. The total area for clearing and planting was a substantial one; the site was exposed and at a high elevation. The belts to remain were ten metres wide and were laid out in such a way as to enclose rectangular planting areas approximately 200 metres by 60 metres, the long sides being in a north to south direction. The shelter given to the new plants was very noticeable, and excellent growth resulted. The variety of herbs that appeared in great density in this sheltered local climate was remarkable.

The way in which edge effect operates is not easy to determine. Degree of insolation and orientation of groups have been referred to. Other factors that may also contribute to the effect are light (as opposed to direct sunshine); the degree of shelter provided by the standing trees; the presence of active mycorrhiza on the living roots; the effect of continuing leaf-fall on the fertility of the upper layers of the soil; and the 'aura' of insect-life and micro-organisms surrounding the standing trees, both above and below soil-level.

In the natural forests of the north temperate zone, where clearings are rarely great, few young plants start their life without being influenced in greater or less degree by edge effect. It is only in extensive clearings, resulting from fire, windblow or the action of man, that it is reduced to a mere fringe round the foot of the remaining forest.

Mixtures. The planting of mixtures of species, as opposed to planting a pure crop, enables the manager to suit the species he selects to the site that he is planting. Blanket-planting of one species denies him this very important silvicultural freedom.

Planting trees in mixtures may also help to give stability to a crop in an area where strong winds can be expected. It will reduce the danger of epidemic disease or insect infestation, through the wider dispersal of the vulnerable species. It permits the use of nurses to assist with the establishment of a more valuable species. It may also lead to an increase in the vigour and production of some species, owing to their interaction and affinity with other species. In economic terms, it provides for earlier returns where conifers are mixed with broad-leaves, and a better spread of marketable products.

A disadvantage of mixtures is that they are not so easily managed. One prescription cannot so conveniently be applied to all the species concerned, whether it is in planting, brashing, thinning, harvesting or marketing. But this disadvantage is largely offset where the Group Selection System is in operation since the management in such cases is essentially more intensive. Mixtures certainly require more care in management but they are also more flexible, providing the forester with more options in the event of disaster to one or more of the species involved.

Planting patterns. In this context the planting of pure crops requires no consideration, but where mixtures are concerned the patterns employed are of great importance. Intimate mixtures of species by single trees are now rarely used, although there are a few well-known traditional patterns such as that used for many years on the Brocklesby Estate in Lincolnshire. It is more usual to plant in pure lines, belts, or groups. Single lines have the disadvantage that, unless the constituent species all grow at the same rate, it is very difficult to avoid damage to the slower-growing trees by those that outstrip them; this implies intensive management, almost certainly involving a very short thinning-cycle.

The two commonest systems employed today are belts and groups. The former system is perhaps most widely used on the grounds that management generally, and extraction in particular, are much simplified. Certainly this may be true if 'management' refers only to the successive removals of whole lines of trees; and on very large plantation areas this method will have a strong appeal. Its disadvantages are that successive line-thinnings progressively reduce selectivity so that bulk is produced at the expense of quality; that more broad-leaved trees are used in belts than in groups and therefore there is a reduced interim yield from the conifer element; and that on hill-slopes the all-too-familiar pattern of 'pyjama-stripes' that results is not attractive to the eye, and may be environmentally unacceptable.

The group system aims at using the minimum number of broad-leaves necessary to produce the required crop, the remainder of the available space being used to grow a matrix of conifers that can be sold profitably as thinnings. In experimental plantings during the period immediately after the last world war the writer used as many as 25 beech plants to form a group. This was reduced progressively as experience suggested, first to 16 and later to nine. In the special case of wild cherry the number was reduced to the ultimate, one cherry being planted at ten metre spacing in larch planted at two metres. This is made possible by the very rapid growth of the cherry when given adequate side-shade.

A more intricate system devised by the late Ray Bourne provided for a larch matrix into which were set groups consisting of five broad-leaves in a diamond pattern, with four strong shade-bearers at the corners, making a square of nine trees. Thus a diamond of five oaks would have four western red cedar set around it to complete the square. This ensured that the oak would be well drawn-up and shaded, despite the light foliage of the larch.

This method involves more intensive management, as does the group method in general, this being justified by the aim, which is the economical production of high quality broad-leaved trees. The economy lies in the reduction in the number of broad-leaves which have little or no value as thinnings, compared with the number of the more saleable conifers that comprise the matrix. A group system, using nine plants to a group and with a matrix of three rows of conifers each way between the groups will require only half as many broad-leaved plants as are required by the belt system; and the number of potentially saleable conifers is increased in proportion.

In stands produced in this way, it is expected that the centre tree of the group will probably emerge as the best-shaped tree; it has been surrounded by trees of the same species, closely spaced, and free during its early years from over-shading by the more aggressively-growing members of the conifer matrix. The first thinning removes the line of conifers on the south or south-west side of the broad-leaved groups, allowing sunlight to reach their developing crowns. A silvicultural thinning of the remainder of the crop is made at the same time.

The group method contains an in-built hedge against complete failure since the conifers are also in groups; so that even if the broad-leaves fail, in part or *in toto*, conifers of high quality can be produced from the original mixture. This is shown in the accompanying diagram, Figure 9.

Nursing. The planting of mixtures of conifers with broad-leaved trees has long been practised, the conifers generally being regarded as a temporary constituent of what is intended to be a final crop of broad-leaved trees. The

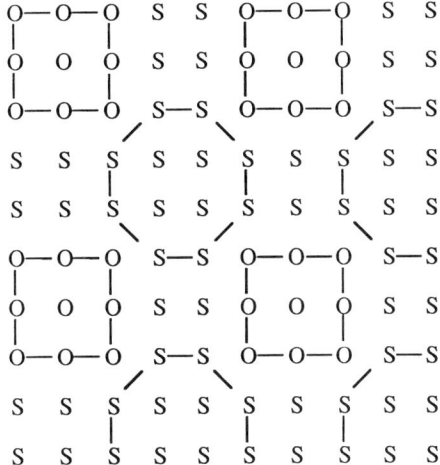

In the diagram, O stands for oak and S for spruce. The distance between the central oaks in adjacent squares is ten metres.

In the diagram, O stands for oak, T for western red cedar, and L for larch. The distance between the central oaks of adjacent squares is ten metres.

Figure 9.

conifers in the initial stages have the function of nurses; they are there to give shelter to the developing broad-leaves and to shade their stems, thus helping to suppress side-branches and encouraging clean straight growth. They also have an important economic function. As the crop develops and the crowns of the broad-leaves require more space, the conifers begin to be removed in successive thinnings, at which stage they have a marketable value. The variants of the system are so familiar in this country that there is a tendency to take its merits for granted.

But on the Continent of Europe it has been common practice for centuries to raise broad-leaves in pure plantings at very close spacing, especially oak; and beech, ash, and sycamore have been grown very successfully in large pure groups in this country. It is clear from this experience that the traditional use of conifers as nurses is not always silviculturally justified; it is in their use as a source of interim cash yields that their real value lies. A plantation of pure broad-leaves provides little value in the form of early thinnings and, in districts remote from hardwood pulp-mills and bulk markets for firewood, their profitable disposal can be a real embarrassment.

This common experience emphasizes once again the folly of paying undue attention to market requirements when designing new plantations. Pure ash designed to provide saleable thinnings for hurdle-making and other traditional agricultural uses is a good example; and the well-known story of the assessment made in 1910 of the estimated hay requirements of the London cab-horses for the next 50 years is as pertinent as ever.

The merits of using certain specialized nurses for purely silvicultural reasons are of course well-recognized and accepted. For example, alder has a special value for its ability to fix atmospheric nitrogen in its root-nodules and therefore to be a positive soil improver. This characteristic, together with the fact that it accepts regular coppicing, gives it a special place among tree nurses. On the one hand it helps to enrich the soil and on the other it can easily be kept under control. By coppicing, its height can be adjusted to suit the needs of the crop-trees.

CHAPTER 15

Planting: Techniques

Preparation for planting. With the ever-increasing cost of labour in relation to the price received for timber sold, it is vitally necessary to ensure that trees planted do not suffer checks to their growth. Any checks, or deaths among the plants, will involve the beating-up of failures and expensive successive weedings until the plants are established and out of danger from weeds and frost. Any steps that can be taken to reduce the burden of after-care should be taken, even though they may add to the initial cost of planting. Such steps may be:

a. Accurate planting in line to facilitate mechanical weeding or inter-row spraying. On small areas the use of a cord to mark out lines has proved economical in this context, permitting very close mowing.

b. Cutting of remaining stumps and stubs to ground-level, for the same reason.

c. Forking of the ground at each plant-site. On compacted gravel on the site of an old army camp in Buckinghamshire, a fork with shortened (and therefore stronger) prongs was used to loosen the soil. One man moved ahead of the planter, opening up the soil and marking the planting point in one operation.

d. Spot- or line-spraying in advance of planting to provide a weed-free medium in which to plant and so to minimize competition for water and nutrients. This is a modern development of the old system of 'screefing', in which the top layer of the soil, with all the weeds growing on it, is removed from the actual planting site before planting begins.

e. Complete ploughing as a means of providing a weed-free planting site, combined with an organically enriched soil. This has been extended to the dressing of the site with well-rotted dung or leaf-mould before ploughing on difficult arable sites, especially in chalk areas.

Intensive measures such as these can be expensive but the cost will often be well repaid by the saving of labour in subsequent years.

Methods of planting. The principle of getting plants away to a good start applies also to the actual planting. Freedom from weed-competition during the first season of growth may be ensured by physical screefing, or by the use of plastic mats or herbicides. There is an additional cost in terms of time and material; but the advantages enjoyed by the plant in reduced competition for water and supplies of essential nutrients during this critical period will well repay the outlay.

The provision of long-lasting supplies of water by dipping the roots in a seaweed solution before planting is another small advantage that can be provided easily and cheaply.

In soils where chalk or limestone is very near the surface, particularly where the planting follows arable crops in such conditions, it is advisable to incorporate some acid material in the planting medium, as mentioned above, in order to counteract the strong effect of the lime. Arable soils on which a succession of cereal crops have been grown tend to be very deficient in organic matter and available minerals. Years of cereal-cropping rapidly reduce these to a level at which annual supplies of nitrogen, phosphorus, and potassium salts have to be provided in the form of artificial fertilizer. These leach out rapidly and leave little in the soil. As far as young trees are concerned, such a site represents an almost sterile medium, compacted and lacking in most of the features characterizing a mature forest soil.

Insufficient attention is often given to the matter of root-direction and future growth. The ploughing technique used in upland planting of conifers is an outstanding example of the victory of convenience over intelligent planning. A method of planting on soils with a high water-table was originally developed in Belgium. A large turf was dug from adjacent ground and inverted on the spot where the plant was to be set. A slot was then cut with a spade down through the inverted turf into the actual soil, and the tree-roots inserted. This ensured that the young tree enjoyed freedom from weed-growth for at least one year, and at the same time provided a double depth of soil in which the plant could spread its roots without reaching water. An additional bonus was that, in the sandwich between the inverted turf and the soil surface, there was a double layer of decaying organic matter. This admirable system produced excellent results, but at the time of its invention there was no efficient means of mechanizing it. The later development of deep-ploughing and planting on the upturned furrow-slice appeared to provide most of the advantages of the Belgian turf system, together with a further perceived advantage in the form of drainage to remove excess water from the upper layers of the soil. In the Belgian system this effect was produced more slowly by the tree roots absorbing it as they developed.

The result of the ploughing techniques is now seen in the crops of trees that have reached the end of their rotation. Many are unstable; in fact, if one were asked to design a system intended to produce unstable trees, one would adopt precisely this method. The trees stand on narrow banks between hollows in which water tends to lie, their roots being restricted by the depth of these hollows, with the result that they can only spread along the banks.

This is of course an extreme example; but the principle applies generally. A tree depends for its stability on its roots. It reacts to the force of the prevailing wind by extending its roots in the direction from which it blows. Any assistance that can be given in the initial alignment of the roots when planting will reduce the expenditure of food materials in developing roots in the right direction. If planting is to be done by digging a hole, then the roots should be spread so that their major part lies along the line of the prevailing wind direction. Where small trees are to be planted in slots or in L- or T-shaped notches, a similar directional alignment should be aimed at; although obviously this cannot be so effectively ensured.

The spraying of patches to be planted and the use of black plastic mats referred to earlier provide additional advantages. Both kill the surface vegetation and so combine the advantages of freedom from weed-competition in the first season of growth and dead turf as a rooting medium with consequent reduced danger from frost, which is greater where the vegetation is grass. Grass loses heat very rapidly by radiation, whereas dead vegetation does not.

Planting in vertical plastic shelters has much to recommend it when used for individual trees, and it has been very effective in carrying them on beyond the point at which they are vulnerable to weed-growth and grazing by deer. However the expense involved, although there is a saving on the cost of fencing and on weeding and immediate after-care, leads inevitably to the adoption of very wide spacings. The subsequent free growth at such spacings is unlikely to produce clean stems, with the resultant need for regular intensive pruning. This will be necessary for a prolonged period and is liable to be overlooked. It is probable that many of the extensive plantings established by this method will fail to produce satisfactory trees owing to the physical impossibility of carrying out all the essential pruning when it becomes necessary.

Direct sowing. A traditional Continental European method of raising broad-leaves has been that of sowing the seed in the forest. This was a common method of establishing oak woods, the acorns being sown in furrows. It was a cheap way of growing oak at the very close spacing that was normally adopted. Since oak has a strong tap-root, which often exceeds the shoot in length during its first year of growth, it grows better when sown *in situ* since this important root is not cut, as it must be when plants are raised in a nursery. Probably the main weakness of the system lay in its use in areas where wild boar were tolerated in the forest as game, since once they discovered the furrows the animals would follow them along and eat all the acorns.

Modifications of this method have been tried on a small scale and have proved effective. These have consisted of dibbling acorns at considerably less density, the spacings used being more akin to those used in conventional planting. Rapid clean growth in the early stages, resembling that of ash seedlings, has been achieved by the planting of four western red cedar or Lawson cypress round each patch of one, three, or four acorns.

It is probable that dibbling of beech seed would be equally successful during heavy mast years when good seed is easily and cheaply obtainable in quantity. Natural regeneration could be assisted in this way, and it has special advantages for beech. Normally in a beechwood much of the mast lies exposed on the leaf-litter where it is easily found by pigeons that consume vast quantities. Moreover, much of what remains fails to survive after germination because the radicle is unable to reach the mineral soil before the food supply provided by the cotyledons is exhausted, owing to the compactness of the litter. Dibbling at once ensures contact with the mineral soil and also creates a disturbance of the litter immediately above the seed. The dibbling of one seed at a spacing of one metre should, when accompanied by the scuffling of the litter resulting from the operator's movements, ensure a very full and successful regeneration. This should prove an economical way of filling in gaps where partial regeneration has already appeared.

Broadcast sowing. This is not normally a viable method; the failure rate is inevitably high. Artificial seeding cannot, axiomatically, approximate to the density that occurs in nature, and results reflect this.

CHAPTER 16
Weeding

The object of weeding being to free a plant from competition, it was traditionally regarded as involving the cutting of growth liable to overtop the plant. This was achieved by cutting with a sickle, or in some areas a scythe. Carried out at the optimum time of year, this was fairly effective. The weeds were cut down to ground-level, and in theory they were no longer able to draw water or nutrients from the soil in competition with the planted tree. Most weed species, however, are able to grow again quite rapidly after such treatment, and the competition at root-level and above is renewed. The only way in which complete freedom could be achieved for the plant was by hoeing. This freedom can be assured today by the application of suitable chemicals.

The cost of weeding can be very heavy on the rich soils of southern Britain, and it can continue for up to seven years. A very wide range of chemical sprays has helped to reduce this burden, their greatest value being in providing a weed-free environment for the first two years. Unfortunately this is not always achieved, and a build-up of chemical can sometimes result from recurrent sprayings.

Poisoning, however, does not allow the flexibility provided by hand-weeding. At a stage when a plant is well up, it may be desirable in certain conditions to provide it with protection from strong, and particularly from drying, winds. In areas where the deer population is unacceptably high it may be essential to retain a dense growth of bramble to restrict their movement. In both cases it has been found essential to cut the high weed just sufficiently to ensure that the leading shoot and the first whorl of branches are free from physical damage by over-topping and to leave the remainder of the weed-growth untouched. This can be done with a sickle or suitable slasher but not by chemical means.

Mechanically-propelled brush-cutters can be very useful as a substitute for hand-weeding, especially where successive weed cuttings are required. This is another sphere where some additional expense at an early stage of the plantation can make a considerable reduction in the cost of subsequent operations. On an estate in Norfolk the planting was carried out with strict attention to the alignment of the plants in both directions, and this enabled mechanical weeding to be done with accurate cross-blocking. No chemicals were used at that time on the estate but the rapid development of the plantations weeded in this way was remarkable.

In forests of the Swiss Jura, where natural regeneration was used in management under the Selection System, it was the custom of the forest staff to carry a suitable knife or light cutting-hook at all times when on patrol in the forest. Whenever a young tree was seen to be infested with honeysuckle or requiring assistance in any way, the man would stop and spend perhaps half a minute in clearing it, or removing a double-leader or whatever was required.

Where hand-weeding is still employed in the woods this kind of attention can be recommended. It is no great labour to carry a pair of secateurs or a pruning-knife in the back pocket and to remove double-leaders or over-large side-shoots from the plants as one passes them. If carried out during weeding, these operations cost very little in extra time or labour; their effect on the growth of the trees can be very rewarding.

The principal benefit of chemical weeding is obtained if treatment is carried out before planting begins. This may be in the form of overall spraying or of spot-spraying. The former is the more economical in time but more expensive in the quantity of chemical used; spot-spraying must necessarily be done by some form of manually-operated sprayer and so is more expensive in labour although there is a considerable economy in the use of the spray itself. However it is done, the effect can be dramatic. Killing the weed-growth, especially the grass, ensures that the plant begins its new life free from any competition for either water, nutrients or light. It also ensures that no further labour need be expended on any form of weeding during the plant's first growing season in the wood. Additional advantages in grass areas are that radiation from the dead material is at a lower level, so reducing the danger of damage by ground frost. There is the additional advantage in that the rotting turf provides a valuable source of food for the plant.

The impact on the environment of chemicals used in forestry weeding is very small when compared with that resulting from the agricultural use of similar compounds. Since tree crops are grown on rotations of not less than 40 years, the period during which the spraying is done — for perhaps three or four years until the plants become established — is a very small percentage of the life of the crop. Spraying is rarely carried out more than once a year and seldom over the whole area. Compared with what is used in farming, therefore, the amount of chemicals used in the woods is very small indeed. Even if there were to be a build-up of chemicals in the soil as a result of the spraying, the total amounts would be very small; spraying would be limited to perhaps three years in every 40-year rotation.

The use of polythene mats to reduce the growth of weeds round planted trees has obvious advantages. They are non-pollutant and are permanent; but only in ideal circumstances. They require to be firmly anchored by having their edges dug into the ground and they are not always effective unless the surface of the soil is first screefed, either manually or chemically, since perennial weeds may grow sideways under the mat or actually penetrate it. In hot summer weather there is also the danger that small plants may suffer from scorching by reflected heat.

In planting varieties of poplar, the use of mulches is recommended. Polythene mats can be used, but the more traditional method is to make use of waste material such as old straw, hay, or weeds cut in the course of other cultural operations. The purpose of mulching is a dual one; to prevent or restrict the growth of weeds that will compete with the poplar's roots in their search for both water and nutrients, and to keep the soil cool and moist while the roots are making their lateral spread. Poplars are greedy feeders and require a great deal of water. To be really effective the mulch should extend over a radius of about two metres and polythene is unlikely to prove economical over this sort of coverage.

CHAPTER 17
Cleaning, Brashing, and De-Wolfing

The term 'cleaning' is traditionally given to the cutting of birch, sallow, and other woody weeds at the stage when herbaceous weeds no longer constitute a threat to the young plants. It is the last operation that can be undertaken to assist them before the side-branches intermesh and prevent access. If action is not taken at this stage, nothing more can be done before the crop is brashed. In practice the most that can be done is to mow or spray between the lines of trees.

Brashing, the removal of branches to a height of about two metres, may take place at any stage of the young plantation prior to thinning; but it is usually deferred until the lower branches are dead or dying and have lost their leaves. However, it is possible to do it at an earlier stage. On a Cheshire estate where pheasant-shooting was an important activity, the operation was carried out almost as soon as the branches of adjacent trees began to touch. This provided advantages from the sporting angle, allowing easier access for the beaters who were thus able to flush all the birds, and also facilitating the business of locating and picking-up the fallen birds. From the forestry angle, although providing easy access during the first season while weed-growth was still suppressed, it encouraged a strong regrowth owing to the greater intensity of light that was able to reach the ground. The one real advantage was that the branches were still of small diameter and could be removed easily and economically.

In advance of full brashing it is important to brash a limited number of inspection racks. This should be done at an early stage after the plantation becomes impenetrable. Its purpose is to allow an assessment to be made of the urgency with which full brashing is required. When the plantation has closed up, it becomes impossible to see whether the trees in the interior are growing satisfactorily or whether they are being over-topped by birch or sallow, or pulled down by heavy bramble growth, honeysuckle, wild clematis or other woody weeds. The inspection racks are made by brashing between two adjacent rows of trees in a rapid operation that adds nothing to the final cost of brashing while giving complete control of the plantation's progress.

The traditional object of brashing, or brushing-up as it used to be called, was to allow access to young tree crops for inspection, and then for marking and thinning. With the adoption of line-thinning techniques there has been a widespread tendency to regard the brashing operation as obsolete. It will be instructive to see how far this attitude is justified.

First, then, if brashing as an operation is omitted from the forestry programme, one may ask at what stage are the lower branches removed from the trees to allow the timber fallers to operate. The answer is that the timber faller has to do it. This is additional to the work that he is normally concerned with in felling, trimming-out, and cross-cutting; and in consequence must be paid for. The expense of brashing is therefore not avoided, although it may be postponed marginally. The actual cost may in fact be higher since the need to brash the tree actually to be felled, while all the surrounding trees remain unbrashed, may present less attractive working conditions than the traditional brashed plantation; the impediment to movement may present safety hazards; and the whole operation is slowed down.

Thus the actual cash saving at the end of the operation is unlikely to be significant enough to justify the loss of the advantages obtained by orthodox brashing. These may be considered under the following heads:

Cleaning. Once the plantation has closed up and become impenetrable, the first opportunity to assess its overall progress is on brashing. Not infrequently, weak patches are found in which woody weeds, such as birch and sallow, have obtained a strong hold. If not cut at this early stage the damage they will cause in suppressing planted trees may seriously prejudice the success of considerable areas of the plantation. Traditionally this cleaning operation was combined with brashing, permitting thorough coverage in one operation. If the cleaning is delayed until the first thinning it may be too late to save the threatened trees; and if the thinnings are sold standing the purchaser will not be interested in assisting with this unremunerative work.

De-wolfing. This is not a traditional operation but it is a very important one, particularly in hardwood crops. Wolf trees (that is, over-large or deformed individuals) invariably assert themselves at an early stage and are easily identifiable when brashing is in progress. If they are felled at this stage the damage caused to neighbouring trees is either greatly reduced or eliminated altogether. If they are left until the first thinning, it is frequently found that they have so damaged the trees around them that the alternatives are to remove them, leaving an unacceptably large gap, or to retain them until a later thinning, to the prejudice of the crop as a whole. At the brashing stage the exploitable value of even the largest wolf is small, and the tree can be left lying at stump, with the avoidance of uneconomic extraction. Although conifer crops will benefit materially from this treatment, it is almost essential in broad-leaved crops where heavy-branched and aggressive wolves can destroy smaller straighter neighbours. One such tree may spoil as many as eight trees growing immediately around it.

Sport. When sport is a consideration, especially pheasant-shooting, plantations become an embarrassment as soon as they close up sufficiently to prevent access by beaters and efficient picking-up behind the guns. Early brashing may well be justified in such circumstances. Unbrashed plantations from which game cannot be flushed are of course useless for shooting, and an important source of income is thereby forfeited.

There is thus a strong case for continuing to brash in an orthodox manner. But as traditionally carried out by hand, it is very labour-intensive and therefore disproportionally expensive. It is probable that the wider spacings now being used in planting to allow the access of a swipe or similar machine for weeding may permit the introduction of new techniques. There seems to be little reason, for example, why a flail mounted on the front of a tractor should not be used economically to reduce the amount of hard-work that is actually necessary.

CHAPTER 18
Pruning

Pruning as part of the weeding operation. Although chemical weeding may be more lasting in effect, more helpful in reducing root-competition and more cost-effective than hand-weeding, it cannot entirely replace it since some assistance is normally required to prevent the planted tree being physically overwhelmed by tall weed not killed out by the spray. While hand-weeding, however limited in intensity, is in progress, the woodman using the hook is in a position to take the first positive step in influencing the shape of the young tree. The early removal of a double-leader will not only help to make a straight tree but it will prevent the wasteful diversion of sugars to unessential parts of the tree and ensure their concentration in the vital selected leader. The result will be more rapid growth in the right direction — upwards, out of further danger from low frost and smothering weed-growth, and into the sunshine. All that is necessary is a pair of secateurs in the belt and an intelligent attitude.

Pruning in group-planting mixtures. At the brashing stage it should be possible to decide which of the nine trees in such a group shows the best potential in terms of shape. This is often a matter of genetics; the tree selected may in fact have a smaller diameter than the others in the group but be straight and clean. The writer has found that a convenient way of marking the selected tree is to prune it clear of branches to half its height.

This clearly identifies the tree in each group that is to be favoured in all future operations. At the same time it promotes top growth by reducing the wasteful expenditure of sugars on low branches. It also ensures the development of knot-free timber in at least part of the valuable butt-length which may eventually become of veneer quality.

Pruning in crops at wide spacing. Trees grown at spacings of three metres or more lack the stimulus to straight clean growth which is provided by the conventional method of crowding young trees together. Trees grown in tree-shelters are usually spaced widely owing to the high cost of the operation, and they will inevitably require successive prunings before the canopy of the crop closes. Not only will they require attention aimed at producing a straight leader; they will also require to have over-large side-branches reduced. The wild cherry provides a good example of such growth. When grown in a close crop, with side branches restricted, the tree is a fast grower and its shape is normal. When open-grown, the cherry tends to develop strong side-branches at a very early stage. Reducing these to half their length concentrates growth on the leading-shoot and helps in the development of a well-balanced tree. These branches are often of considerable thickness at the base (that is, the point at which they leave the main stem) and it is not advisable to cut them back to this point owing to the disproportionate size of the scar that is produced. It is sufficient to reduce the branch to half-length, which restricts its production of leaves and therefore its rate of growth. The diameter of the side-branch becomes proportionally smaller as the main stem develops, and the wound, when eventual pruning is done to clean the stem, is relatively small and heals easily.

Pruning of epicormic shoots. This has been found to be necessary and effective with oak grown on the free-growth system. It has also been mentioned earlier in connection with oak standards in the application of the coppice-with-standards system. Such pruning is not necessarily final, and further shoots may appear in subsequent years. Indications suggest that the removal of the dormant buds themselves is the essential requirement, rather than the cutting of the more obvious growth. It would seem, therefore, that such removal should be done early in the tree's life when a flush cut can be achieved; a pruning-chisel is probably the ideal tool. Cutting of epicormic twigs with secateurs is likely to be a waste of time, and pruning with a saw would have to be very close indeed to have any lasting effect. Sprays that retard the development of buds have shown some promise but the ideal solution to the oak-epicormic problem undoubtedly lies in the selection of the appropriate genetic strains.

High pruning. High pruning is a proved and effective way of producing high quality timber from butt-lengths. It has been developed to a high degree of perfection in Germany where clear lengths of slowly-grown Scots pine have traditionally commanded high prices. It is, however, a laborious and therefore expensive business, despite the development of various ingenious machines. If the job is necessary to achieve the valuable timber lengths, it must be done properly and carefully; and this means ladder-work for any length greater than six metres. Poplar, with its very wide spacing, is a special case, and pruning in these crops has, on large areas, been brought to a high standard of efficiency by the use of chain-saws operated from hydraulically-lifted platforms. These refinements are rarely available in the case of orthodox tree crops.

Healthy trees making normal growth are able to heal pruning wounds efficiently and fairly rapidly by covering them with callus-tissue. The wound should not normally exceed about eight centimetres in diameter, which ensures that no heartwood has developed and allows a covering of callus-tissue to appear before fungus rot or insect borer attack develops in the exposed wood.

The cost of high pruning can only be recouped if the timber can be sold eventually at a higher than normal price as 'clear of knots'. For this to be achieved the work must be undertaken successively while the diameter of the section treated is still small, beginning ideally when it is no more than eight centimetres. The other essential is that the operation should be recorded so that the timber can in due course be offered for sale as certified free of knots. A scheme was introduced by the Timber Growers Organization many years ago under which a grower could have his crop inspected after pruning and be given a certificate to that effect.

It is often said that high pruning is not worth the effort. But for a landlord who takes an interest in his woods there is much to be said for it. The satisfaction given by a fine stand of pruned trees may be rated very highly indeed.

Tree pruning should ideally be carried out in late summer when the sap-flow is at a reduced level but growth is still continuing. At this time callus-formation will enable the edges of the new wound to be protected before hard winter frosts occur, which can damage the exposed tissues. If there are reasons why the pruning has to be carried out at some other time of the year, the spring and early summer should be avoided owing to the heavy sap-flow.

Protection of pruning scars. The traditional method was to apply Stockholm tar or a good lead paint to the wound when this was dry. The use of commercial sealants has come under criticism in recent years owing to the danger of sealing in moisture, and current recommendations are to the effect that wounds should be left unprotected. This is normally satisfactory on oak and some other trees on which the wounds remain sound until covered by the new callus-tissue. In beech, sycamore and birch, wounds of anything but the smallest size are liable to early attack by wood-boring insects if left unprotected. Since fashions change rapidly with the development of new products, it is recommended that a manager undertaking extensive pruning should consult a horticultural institute in an apple-growing area.

CHAPTER 19
Thinning: Basic Considerations

It is unusual in forestry practice to plant only the trees that will form the final crop. This type of husbandry is only normally seen in what are regarded as horticultural crops, such as orchards, or in tropical plantation crops such as rubber or oil-palms. Forestry, aiming at the production of straight clean trees capable of being converted into useful timber, normally requires the trees to be grown in close association, both to encourage them to grow straight and also to make full use of the available ground. Because so many more trees are planted, or produced by natural seeding, than are required in the final crop, the removal of the majority is necessary before the end of the rotation in order to provide space for the crowns and root-systems of the final trees to expand. The stages and rates at which this is done vary within a very wide range. What are known as 're-spacing' and 'oceanic' regimes require the opening-up of tree-crops as soon as the crowns begin to touch; whereas 'no-thinning' regimes provide for the growing to full rotation age of all the trees planted, like a crop of cereals.

Root-competition. Thinning is required at certain definite stages in the growth of a crop of trees to enable them to spread their crowns, as we have seen. This is in order that they can produce more leaves and so increase the photosynthetic capacity and therefore their food supply. It is not always remembered that the root-system must also be able to expand in proportion. A tree growing in the open without competition, for example in a park, will normally have a root-system that extends well beyond the limits of its crown.

In the forest, where trees are growing in close company with their neighbours, the root-systems must inevitably interlock with each other. This implies severe competition for water and nutrients. Where the crop is of one species, all the trees will have exactly similar requirements in this respect; the competition will be more intense than in the case of mixtures where the various species present will make somewhat different demands on the soil, probably at different levels. This may be in respect of the nutrients themselves or in the actual depth from which they are drawn. A surface-feeding tree, such as beech, may well grow more satisfactorily in company with ash feeding at a greater depth than as a pure crop.

The competition for nutrients is also a factor in the 'sickness' of soils. Some beechwoods in the Chilterns are said to be 'beech-sick' when the trees do not appear to be growing as rapidly as could reasonably be expected. On thin clay-with-flints soils over chalk, the drain on the limited supply of nutrients made by a succession of pure beech crops over the centuries may well be responsible for the present appearance of such areas. 'Sickness' of the soil under successive crops of conifers in some Continental European forests may be due to similar causes. This particularly refers to conifers such as spruce, where the formation of raw humus occurs, and the re-cycling of the nutrients is delayed. At the same time the rotations on which such crops are grown are much shorter than those employed for beech, and the volume of timber harvested, both in final fellings and in thinnings, is much greater. The loss of nutrients over a period of several rotations is therefore likely to exceed by a considerable margin that resulting from the growing of beech.

Crown damage. 'Whips' (excessively tall thin stems) are recognized as a danger in young crops and are normally removed during the early thinnings. Crown damage among larger and older trees is often not identified, nor its extent appreciated; but it is nevertheless of considerable importance in certain species of broad-leaved trees. This is particularly so in the case of ash. This species suffers severely from bacterial canker which is highly infectious. The writer's attention was drawn to this many years ago by observing some young self-sown ash, between half a metre and one metre in height, growing along the roadside boundary of an ashwood. Growth of bramble at this point was very strong and the young ash growing up through it had become badly scratched, resulting in minor wounds. These were infected with the characteristic cankers of the disease.

During successive thinnings in a Yorkshire ashwood over a period of some 40 years it has been the practice to remove as many trees showing signs of this disease as possible without prejudicing the success of the crop as a whole. Inevitably, some infected trees have been left; and at each successive thinning it has been observed that the numbers have built up again. Observation shows that, in an ashwood, the outer twigs and light branches of the crown move easily in the wind and 'thrash' together. This can cause damage to the crown of a single tree or it can result in mutual damage to two or more adjacent trees. In all such cases the wounds become infected if there are any diseased trees in the crop, and spread of the disease is inevitable. Very severe thinning of infected young ash crops at an early stage, aiming at the complete removal of sources of infection, is therefore essential.

Shading of the stem. Thinning results in an increase of light falling on the stems of the remaining trees. It also provides space for the crown to expand. Both these factors are involved in the way the trees respond to thinning and the intensity with which it is applied. Shading of the stems of broad-leaved trees is important, not only as an aid to the suppression of epicormic shoots but for another reason as well. In natural virgin forest, simulated in large patches of natural regeneration, most broad-leaved trees grow in intense competition, generally with trees of the same species. In their early years the bark is not exposed to strong sunlight and heat in the summer, and in winter it is protected from very intense cold by mutual crowding. As a result it will be found that such trees, often up to six metres in height, will have a very thin outer bark. This may be seen particularly clearly in young ash that is growing very rapidly in optimum conditions. On such trees a light scratching of the outer bark with the finger-nail will reveal the bright green inner layer. At this stage the bark is growing rapidly and expanding, exerting the minimum constricting effect on the fast-growing sap-wood below it. It is common experience to see longitudinal cracks in the bark of young ash, indicating rapid growth. But when the bark is only paper-thin there is no need for the bark to split. The very fact of splitting indicates tension; with very thin bark this does not exist; the growth is free.

The opposite side of the coin is seen in the fruit-grower's technique of releasing young trees from the effect of bark-binding by making a vertical slit with a knife from the first branch down to ground-level. This at one stroke releases the tension in the bark and the pressure on the cambium and outer layers of the sap-wood; and at the same time it induces the formation of 'pipes' of new callus-tissue at the lips of the resulting crack, along which the sap can flow freely. A bark-bound tree is the very opposite of one in which the bark offers no constraint to the expansion of the tree's growth.

Trees grown in a close crop, even though they may have passed the stage at which the bark is thin and soft, often suffer if suddenly exposed to strong sunlight. This is seen when beech, which is particularly prone to this damage, is exposed by the felling of an adjacent coupe. On south-facing boundaries such trees may lose considerable patches of bark through overheating, leading to the death of the bark-tissues; and lesser damage, although insufficient to kill the bark, may allow the entry of pathogens, resulting ultimately in the familiar 'beech-bark disease' syndrome.

Reference has been made earlier to the introduction of shade-bearing conifers into group-patterns intended to produce oak trees of high quality. In addition to the nursing effects in suppressing side-branches and forcing up the tree as a straight stem, this system also ensures the protection of the bark of the oak trees during the important juvenile period. Western red cedar and Lawson cypress both grow very well alongside oak. Any individuals that compete too strongly can be removed; while the less vigorous ones, those partially suppressed by the crowns of the oak, remain as a more or less permanent sub-dominant element, continuing to shade the oak stems for perhaps 40 years or more. At the same time, they reduce the light penetrating to the forest floor and restrict the growth of plants which would otherwise compete for water and minerals. Their own leaf-fall is comparatively small, and the resultant leaf-litter is predominantly of oak.

Ring width. The rate of growth of a tree depends largely on the size of its crown and, where the tree is an individual constituent of a crop, this will be reflected in the degree to which the crop is thinned. One of the criteria in the quality of timber grown in temperate climates is the width of the annual rings. In tropical evergreen forest, growth-rings as such do not appear; but in the species with which we are concerned here the differential width of the rings is of great importance. This is sometimes stated in clear terms in the specifications supplied by buyers of timber for specialized purposes. Thus 'sports ash', used variously at one period in the construction of articles requiring the maximum degree of flexibility, had to comply with a specification of between six and eight rings to 25 millimetres measured along the radius. Hoops or rings by which the sails of fishing-boats were attached to the mast and spars were also traditionally made of ash, and for these the specification was a very tight one, requiring both a maximum and minimum width for the rings and also limiting their differential distribution. These are extreme examples. In the case of quality timber, it is important that the width of the rings should be even. This is governed essentially by the thinning, which determines the rate of growth. It will be noted, however, that an even rate of growth throughout the rotation will not result in the production of wood with rings of even width; for, as the diameter and girth of the tree increase, the rings produced by the same amount of wood become progressively narrower. To obtain timber with rings of even width it is therefore necessary to slow down the growth of the tree in its early youth and to accelerate it in its later life.

In terms of silvicultural treatment this implies a restriction of the crown in the early pre-thinning and early thinning stages, with steady regular freeing of the crown thereafter to permit maximum expansion up to rotation age, as in the application of the Selection System. Failure to control the ring-width in this way produces the familiar effect so often observed in the butts of Japanese larch (*Larix kaempferi*) and in many broad-leaves — wide rings at the centre, resulting from vigorous juvenile growth, followed by increasingly narrower rings, widening periodically as successive thinnings allow the crown to expand again, grow more leaves and produce more wood by increased photosynthetic activity.

Seed-bearers of weed-trees. The presence of birch and sallow seedlings in a young crop of trees can result in considerable expense in weeding, or even in complete failure of the crop. Conifer crops can, in certain circumstances, stand overall spraying, and so present few problems in this respect; but broad-leaved crops are not open to any such simple treatment. Once the birch and sallow get a hold, only regular mechanical weeding or spraying down the rows will hold them in check. And this is only a temporary effect. After mowing, these weed-trees will shoot again strongly with the added stimulus given by coppicing; and neither mowing nor chemical weeding will remove every individual weed standing between the plants in the line or immediately adjacent to the planted trees.

Where circumstances permit, therefore, and especially in an economic climate where there is a sale for firewood or pulpwood, action should be taken to carry out a deliberate thinning of older broad-leaved woodland adjacent to new planting areas, limiting the cutting to birch and sallow, all of which should be removed. Ideally this operation should cover a wide radius since the seed of birch is very light indeed and can be carried by the wind for long distances. This thinning should be done well in advance of any proposed felling and re-stocking; where there is a five-year management plan it could well be programmed to take place five years prior to the felling.

This form of protection is not 100 per cent effective, however, since the seed has been found to lie in the ground and remain viable longer than is suggested by current research. It does, however, offer a positive means of reducing the danger of birch and sallow infestation of planting areas.

CHAPTER 20
Thinning: Techniques

Free growth. Natural regeneration, which often appears in great density, cannot be treated according to the orthodox systems devised for planted trees. Small areas provide few treatment problems. Cautious thinning-out at an early stage can be followed by successive thinnings at intervals suggested by the rate of growth until a spacing similar to that employed in planted crops is attained. Thereafter the regimes prescribed for the latter may be followed.

Large areas, on the other hand, require a quite different approach. In an area of natural regeneration of broad-leaves, stems of about one metre in height may stand at less than 30 centimetres apart, or 108,875 to the hectare. The very density precludes opening to, say, one metre apart in one operation, since the young trees are mutually drawn and have insufficient strength to stand if unsupported by their fellows. An initial opening to, say, 60 to 90 centimetres is necessary, followed by a second thinning, giving a spacing of perhaps 1.5 to 2 metres by which time the stems may well be 3 metres tall. Thus at least two, and in many cases three, thinnings are necessary before the stage corresponding to the first thinning of a planted crop is reached. During these preliminary thinnings some 105,000 stems per hectare have to be cut; and these operations can be expensive and a severe drain on manpower.

On the Continent of Europe, where natural regeneration methods are traditional, the problem was generally solved in the past by permitting peasants to cut the unwanted sticks for fuel. Where the faggot is still in use and where an inherited forest sense among forest-dwellers guarantees a satisfactory operation, this provides an ideal solution. In Britain and other countries lacking either or both these conditions, other methods must be found.

Belgian thinning. The system described below was suggested by a compromise employed in some Belgian forests where the forest staff simply free the crowns of a number of selected stems from immediate competition and ignore the remainder. This is satisfactory for small areas, but where the crop to be treated extends over a very large area it is clear that a somewhat more systematic method is required.

The following method of treatment was devised to deal with the very large areas of ash and sycamore regeneration resulting from the system adopted on a Gloucestershire estate for the rehabilitation of its war-devastated woodlands. It is based on the assumption that the aim is to produce mature trees with a crown-diameter of ten metres, and it can be applied in natural regeneration from 2.5 metres and upwards in height.

A team consists of two men with a small chain-saw, a bill-hook, a pot of white paint and a pot of yellow paint. A suitable base-line is selected, for example a straight ride forming a boundary of the compartment. A stem is selected arbitrarily about five paces inside the crop at right-angles to this line, and it is painted with a white band at eye-level. This is the 'marker'. The two best stems are now selected within a radius of five paces of this marker, and are banded with yellow paint. They must be far enough apart to allow each to develop at least to pole-size without mutual interference. Each yellow-banded tree is now freed from immediate competition by felling surrounding stems to give a full 1.5-metre clearance all round the crown.

The men then walk ten paces from the marker, parallel to the base-line, and they paint the nearest stem with a white band, as a second marker. Markers may be of any species and any shape; their function is simply to permit an even gridding of the area. The two best trees within five paces are again selected for painting with yellow bands, and their crowns freed as before. The men continue, sighting back along their markers to ensure that their line is straight, until they come to the boundary. They then pace a distance of ten metres at right-angles to their previous line, and come back along a line parallel to it and ten metres distant. In this way two good stems are selected and given room to grow for every ten metre square, thus providing two candidates from which to select the final-crop tree at a later date.

Dry weather is necessary for satisfactory adhesion of the paint and for the woodmen's comfort, and best results are obtained when the leaf is off. Under these conditions two men can cover about 0.75 hectares a day in ash and sycamore, 3 to 3.5 metres in height, where the ground is reasonably clear of bramble and other heavy weed-growth.

This system permits the final-crop trees to be safeguarded when labour is not available to carry out intensive operations. If, however, labour becomes available at a later date and the produce should be saleable, then it is possible to return to the treated crop and to thin it in a more orthodox manner, provided that the stems of the selected trees are not exposed by cutting near them.

The system can be extended very simply for application to young crops that have reached the stage at which they are due for conventional silvicultural thinning. Since first, and often second, thinnings are rarely valuable enough to be worth marketing, a method that calls for the minimum of labour and time, while ensuring the welfare of the final crop trees may be of very great value.

In planted crops, the gridding of the area is much simplified. The operators walk along the appropriate rows that provide a ten metre spacing, painting markers and selecting the best two stems within each square as indicated above. For trees of this size it will generally be necessary to free the crowns sufficiently to give a full 1.5 metre clearance all round. In mixed crops, a clear indication will be required of the relative priority to be given to each species when selecting trees to be favoured.

In scrub areas where there is a fair scattering of potential timber trees, the system can be employed to ensure that the best possible use is made of the available elements. In such situations the matrix of hazel and other low growth will serve a very useful purpose in keeping the stems of the selected trees well shaded and so relatively free of epicormic shoots. Crops of this kind, at first sight not worthy of retention, may, if treated in this way, eventually produce large-headed trees with comparatively short boles of veneer quality and high value.

The advantages of the system are that:

1. It permits areas to be treated that would otherwise have to be left too long, or would never be taken in hand at all.
2. It allows the selected trees to grow with free crowns but with their stems surrounded by their crowded fellows, ensuring clean stems and a shaded forest-floor.
3. It ensures an even distribution of favoured stems.
4. It is efficient in that the selected trees are marked indelibly and not lost sight of.
5. It facilitates the periodical freeing of the crowns of the selected trees, which are easily identified.
6. It is cheap to operate.
7. It can be used to establish broad-leaved crops where there is an even distribution of young saplings among hazel, without need for the complete clearance of the latter.
8. It reduces the risk of damage to the best trees where grey squirrels are active by providing a large number of alternative trees of small value. With orthodox thinning techniques the latter are removed, which focuses attention on a decreasing number of superior trees.

Stick thinning. In a dense crop of broad-leaved trees, in which neither the free-growth nor Belgian system is being employed, the marking of the trees to be removed in a thinning can be both laborious and expensive. On the assumption that there is a local market for firewood, a possible solution can be to sell the thinnings standing, at an agreed stacked-measure price at roadside, all the work of felling and extraction being done by the purchaser. Provided that the operation is an early one and that there is little to choose between the stems as to quality, the spacing can be controlled by using a stick to limit the spacing. The contractor's operator soon accustoms himself to the technique, which is to choose a good tree at random and with this as centre to swing an appropriate-sized stick in a circle. Any tree that the stick touches may be cut. Another good tree on the perimeter of this circle is selected for retention, and the process continues. It will be found that a two-metre stick will result in an approximate spacing of 2.75 metres between the trees left standing after completion of the thinning. This system is specially suitable in areas where the operators have no inherited woodland skills.

With a brush-cutter the system can be applied in patches of very young natural regeneration where there is no market for the small produce. In this case the sweep of the brush-cutter will determine the spacing.

Pre-swiping. There are considerable advantages to be obtained by clearing bracken and bramble before beginning to mark the thinning. With woodmen using chain-saws it is important that there should be as little as possible in the way of loose growth to impede their progress while carrying these heavy machines, or to 'snatch' at them while in use. A man should be able to step backwards with safety when the tree begins to fall. It is obviously good policy to make his working conditions as safe as possible.

If swiping of the weed-growth is to be done for the benefit of the woodmen, advantage should be taken of this additional expense to make life easier also for the forester who marks the thinning. This implies that the swiping should be done before marking begins. The difference to the marker can be a very considerable saving in time and labour. Breasting bracken up to two metres high or bramble up to the knees can be a very exhausting business, and the fatigue involved inevitably reduces efficiency. As an extreme example the writer remembers one occasion when it took him ten minutes to cut his way through very high bramble from one big oak to the next one.

Where the wood concerned forms part of a shooting estate, swiping may be done in lines in the direction in which the wood will be driven. Provided that a completely clear floor is not left, this will be to the mutual advantage of both the woods and the game departments. Where these considerations do not apply, swiping is best carried out in the general direction of the planting lines, as this greatly assists the man who is doing the marking.

Marking strategy. There are two main approaches to the question of how to set about marking for thinning. In young plantations where the trees are still densely spaced, there is a good deal to be said for walking along the lines, since this helps to avoid the overlooking of any patches. However, this advantage is far outweighed on sloping ground by the disadvantages of having to look upwards at an increased angle if the lines are so orientated as to make this necessary.

The other method is to start at the bottom of the slope and to walk along the contour, marking the trees on their uphill sides. On reaching the edge of the compartment one climbs up the slope for a distance equal to the spacing of, say, four or five trees, and walks back along the contour. At this and all subsequent stages the trees already marked will be clearly visible below. At the same time, owing to the slope, the crowns of the trees being inspected will be at a lower angle of sight. This reduces fatigue and avoids the reduction of blood-flow to the brain that can become a limiting factor when marking large areas, even on level ground. This may be serious, resulting in a break in the automatic rhythm of steady marking that one develops, and leading to hesitations and doubts. When this occurs, a rest is indicated, and it is recommended that should one stand for five or ten minutes with neck bent and eyes on the ground.

Marking for thinning. The traditional method of marking for thinning was by using a scribe or by blazing with a bill or hand-axe. The scribe, very similar to the instrument used for paring horses' hooves, cuts a thin line in the bark; a double line, cut obliquely to the vertical, shows up well on the thin bark of young smooth-barked trees and satisfactorily, though not so clearly, on older trees of these species. But it does not show up so well on older trees with rough bark.

Blazing is satisfactory for all species of tree, provided that the felling is to take place within a reasonable time. On young ash, beech, and sycamore the blaze-wounds will callus over within the space of a year or two, dependent on the depth of the cut; where only the bark is removed, healing will take place very rapidly on fast-growing trees, and the mark will then only be visible at short range. In the case of conifers, the flow of resin consequent on the cutting of the blaze will often obscure the mark, and will sometimes cause confusion by producing a whitish patch of dried resin resembling a painted spot or a natural wound.

Paint is commonly used, applied either by brush or by spray. Both methods have their limitations and special advantages. Brush-painting provides a clear mark, easily distinguishable, and is more likely to be permanent where the bark is damp; the spray is more easily applied. Brush-painting should only be done with non-drip paints as otherwise the forester will inevitably get paint on his hands and clothes. It is not so much drip from the brush that does the damage as the unavoidable touching or dripping onto small branches that then pass it on to one's clothes. Sprays are expensive since one charge of paint will only treat a limited number of trees. Both are extremely uncomfortable operations since the hands are more or less fixed in one position for long periods during the cold weather that normally obtains when marking is done, when the leaf is off. On the whole, hand-painting with non-drip paint is preferable; with reasonable care the paint-pot can be carried under the arm, allowing one hand to rest in the pocket. The other hand, gloved and carrying the brush, will be in fairly constant motion. This may appear to be a small matter, but reasonable comfort is essential if the job is to be done efficiently. A long stint of marking makes considerable demands on a man's stamina, with brain and body working at full stretch.

Wind-rowing brush. A method sometimes adopted, particularly on traditional shooting estates, is that of piling the brush in tidy wind-rows between every second or third line of trees. This makes for easier working as felling of the marked thinnings proceeds, and makes access for beaters much easier during the shooting season. It is also safer for the woodmen since they are continually providing a cleared working area for themselves. On the other hand it involves more time and labour and is therefore more expensive; and the rows of brushwood provide safe potential harbourage for rabbits. For subsequent access to the plantation, except along the cleared lines, the rows of brushwood constitute a serious obstacle; and this becomes particularly inhibiting to the forester marking the next cyclical thinning since the brush is unlikely to have rotted down within a five-year period. There are further problems when the extraction of thinnings begins, since movement of the felled material across the lines of heaped brushwood becomes very difficult indeed, whether this is to be done by hand or by winch.

Thinning by poisoning. There are some circumstances in which thinning becomes necessary for the health and growth of a crop of trees in a situation where there is no market for the material to be cut. The cheapest and most labour-saving way of dealing with this problem is to kill the trees that would normally be felled and to leave them standing. When they die, their neighbours will grow on past them, using the additional crown-space thus made available. Killing the trees can be done most effectively by poisoning, a suitable poison solution being injected either under pressure or by pouring it into a 'frill-girdle'. The latter is made by chopping round the stem with an oblique axe-cut so that the cut bark stands out as a frill, leaving a channel for the reception of the poison.

Thinning with an oblique cut. In similar circumstances a comparable result can be obtained by cutting the tree that is to be 'removed' with an oblique cut at about two metres from the ground with a light chain-saw. The upper part of the tree will drop until its base touches the ground. It will remain vertical owing to the contact of adjoining tree crowns. The effect of this is to kill the tree and to give immediate release to the upper two metres of the crowns of its neighbours.

CHAPTER 21
Felling

Timing of felling. It was traditional practice to limit felling to the winter months when the leaf was off, implying that the sap was no longer running in the trees, and this is still generally observed. The reason for it was primarily that a log containing the minimum of sap would season more rapidly when exposed to the air, and that it would be less liable to be attacked by fungi and wood-boring beetles because it contained less sugar. An additional advantage was that broad-leaves and larch carried no leaves at this time of year; this meant that there would be less weight when the tree fell and a consequently reduced danger of its splitting on contact with the ground. There would also be less trouble in clearing and in burning-up the brush, if this was required.

The soundness of this basic reasoning may well be questioned. A sycamore or birch tree whose stem is exposed to full sunlight on a bright day in January will often pour with sap if cut into. On the other hand, the late Lord Bolton, an acknowledged sycamore expert, observed that the flow of sap in sycamore is at its lowest during the month of August. This appears to be confirmed by the writer's own experience over many years.

However, there are risks in summer-felling, as can be seen from the way in which ash is liable to split if felled at this time. This tree is always prone to splitting if the stem has grown away from the vertical, at any season; and it was formerly the practice when dealing with such trees to bind them with chains, windlassed tight, just above the sawing point.

Direction of felling. In a clear-fall, felling should be against the direction of the prevailing wind whenever possible. That is, if the wind is normally from the south-west, felling should begin at the north-eastern side of the coupe and be extended evenly towards the south-west. In reasonably still weather this will put the least strain on the trees being felled and so reduce their liability to split; and it will also avoid the sudden exposure to high winds of each new salient of trees, unprotected by their fellows and with roots not adjusted to sudden strains. In addition, the trees being felled will fall either with or across the wind, thus assisting the fallers in controlling them. This is important in avoiding breakages caused by trees falling across others already on the ground.

In Group Selection working, where group clearances are being made in preparation for natural regeneration of planting, it is important that felling should be carried out in such a way that the heads of the trees fall into the area to be cleared and not into the surrounding woodland, which might result in damage to the crowns and stems of the trees to be left standing. This can usually be achieved fairly simply by selecting one tree that will fall easily in the required direction. This will provide increased space into which the next tree will fall; and each successive tree felled will make the work easier. This implies that the trimming-out of each tree should be completed before the next one falls. If this is done, extraction of the timber is simplified, topwood can be corded, and brush burnt up in the cleared space without any danger of scorch to the standing trees surrounding the cleared area.

Height of stumps. During the last few decades the relation of wages to the value of timber has changed so greatly that it has become less acceptable to insist that trees be cut flush to the ground so that the very last centimetre of usable timber is brought to account. In felling large trees before the last war it was a matter of pride among old-established timber merchants to cut the stumps flush in this way. Such careful work was, in fact, demanded by the owners of large estates, mainly for appearance but also to allow the unrestricted passage of vehicles and machines, not to mention valuable blood-stock. The 'rounding-up' of such large trees was a lengthy and serious business with the axe. Today, with chain-saws, the only problem is getting the saw low enough to the ground; the actual cutting is swift and easy, although there are some snags. At ground level very old trees may contain stones that have fallen into clitches long overgrown, and there may be nails or pieces of wire. When axes were used for this preliminary work, these obstructions were dealt with easily and with no danger. When encountered by a chain-saw they present serious hazards.

In the woods, as opposed to parkland and hedgerows, stumps are now rarely cut very low to the ground unless the trees are very large and valuable; but they should be as low as possible without there being any need for the faller to cut away the soil. Since vehicles will be used in extracting the timber, and machine-weeding may be employed in the subsequent crop of trees planted on the site, it is important that no remaining stumps should be high enough to obstruct these operations.

Brush. After clear-felling it is normally the practice to clear all the brush by burning. But modern methods of 'scarifying', combined with the planting of individually-protected trees at wide spacing, are likely to supersede to a great extent this costly and in many ways wasteful practice. And brush does have several favourable effects. It eventually adds to the organic content of the soil on rotting down. It gives low cover from wind, with appreciable improvement to the micro-climate (one has only to lie down in it on a moderately windy day to appreciate the difference it makes). It tends to discourage the free-ranging grazing habits of deer, and it provides cover for birds, including pheasants.

If retained, the brush should be lightly spread to give a fairly even coverage of the exposed ground. Besides the advantages already mentioned, this gives early protection to young natural seedlings. Where ground cover is not required or where bramble is present, it is preferable to stack the brushwood round the bases of standing trees, leaving the maximum area of ground clear for regeneration or planting. The bramble can then be dealt with by spraying.

In woods being thinned, the clearing of brush is unusual, although it is done on some estates where appearance is considered important or where the shooting interest requires it. In the Chilterns it used to be the practice for timber merchants, or the firewood merchants whom they employed to take away the tops, to burn up the brush. This inevitably resulted in considerable damage to the remaining trees since a hot fire will boil the sap of a beech or other thin-barked tree. No damage was immediately visible, and the merchant was safely away and had probably forgotten the wood three years later when the bark began to fall off the trees standing round the sites of the fires.

Topping of big trees. The value of a very large oak tree with a butt of veneer quality may well justify the cost of removing its crown before felling. As an example, one such tree, with a clear butt of some seven metres' length and a diameter of two metres, had a very large and spreading crown with heavy branches radiating equally all round. No removal of the crown was done prior to felling, and when it came down the tree split longitudinally into several pieces owing to the impact of the large branches on the ground. In consequence its value was reduced very greatly and no veneer timber was recovered. This was of course an exceptional case, but many a fine tree is spoiled as a result of its falling on one large limb. In a clear-fall a skilled workman can usually avoid this but in thinning old woods, where the choice of direction of fall is limited, the danger of splitting a fine stem is ever present.

CHAPTER 22

Extraction

Ideally, there should be easy access to a hard road from any site where trees are to be felled; and indeed figures and distances have been calculated for a wide range of circumstances. These are, however, so varied in practice that they can only be useful when applied over large areas and for specific purposes.

The basic principles are simple enough. To keep the power required to move timber as low as possible, extraction should be downhill where circumstances permit. To keep the time required to the minimum, the distance between felling-site and motorable road should be as short as possible. And for both these reasons the terrain to be covered should be free from obstacles.

Ideally, a hard road or dry extraction ride should touch the perimeter of each sub-compartment at one point at least. Again ideally, this should run along the lower boundary.

Racks. These may be described as intra-woodland extraction rides. They are best aligned to provide an oblique outlet to the boundary-ride or extraction road, but this will generally be determined by the direction of the planting lines. This does not of course apply in natural regeneration areas where the alignment will be arranged to suit local conditions.

The creation of racks, usually by the removal of one row of trees at regular intervals, will begin at an early stage in a crop's life. In broad-leaved woodland in England and Wales the first racks will probably be made to assist beaters to move pheasants out to flushing points. Others will be necessary for inspection purposes, to allow the manager to examine the condition of the young crop, to see whether patchy failures have resulted in a strong growth of birch or sallow that requires to be removed by early cleaning or brashing. It is important therefore that the racks are cut in the right direction; this implies careful early planning of the plantation, beginning with the direction of the planting lines.

The frequency with which racks are made will depend again on a number of factors. Racks at too wide intervals are useless to the shooting manager, as beaters walking along them will inevitably leave untouched islands in the intervening spaces. Although these racks will only be brashed and no trees actually cut at this stage, it is very probable that they will form the basis of the extraction-rack system that is later adopted. The development of this system will depend on whether a line-thinning regime is intended for the first thinnings.

Where the planting is in groups, as in the Group Selection System, the racks will lead to the main extraction route, either directly or by way of minor rides. The main route will be the track used during the extraction of timber felled to create the group. All thinnings will then be removed along this system of racks and rides, with the minimum of damage or disturbance to the surrounding woodland.

Roads. These can vary very widely in character, from lightly stoned rides to full tarmacadam surfaces. It is the 'home-made' roads that it is proposed to deal with here. Too often such roads have resulted from the filling of pot-holes in the rides with rough stone, with the gradual development of rutted, inefficient, and unsuitable tracks that are expensive to maintain, even at a low level. The principal fault is usually in starting the construction too late; the old ride formation is used until the soil is puddled and deep tracks have filled with water.

The decision to build a road should be made as early as possible, and the initial work of grading and drainage carried out while the basic formation is dry and undamaged. The most usual fault after this stage lies in not confining the spread of the road-metal. Such roads are normally only intended to take one line of traffic, adequate passing points being provided. There is therefore no purpose in making the surface wider than that necessary to accommodate one tractor or timber-lorry. To dump road-metal and then to spread it before suitable kerbs have been laid out is inefficient and wasteful. The effect is to produce a minimum depth of metal at the points of maximum wear, resulting in a wide spread and banking-up of metal along the sprawling edges. Large pieces of stone, logs, or even just deeply-cut earth faces should be provided at the limits of the width decided upon and the metal spread between these kerbs. Not only will this prevent the unnecessary spread of the road; it will increase the depth of the metal at the points where it is needed. It will also result in the more economical use of the available metal, thus increasing the length of road that can be made with a given quantity of this expensive item.

The drainage of roads is vital to their successful use. On slopes it can generally be dealt with by grading so that water will run in towards the hill where a channel will form. Shallow open drains cut obliquely into the road-surface at frequent intervals will carry the accumulated water across the road and down the bank. The cross-drains should be lined on either side with a single round pole, the top of which is flush with the road surface, the poles being held firmly in place by iron dogs joining them at suitable intervals and holding them apart. These drains should be self-clearing, only requiring periodical attention. On level ground, roadside drains and the maintenance of effective camber are vitally important.

Road systems on new plantation areas present special problems, the principal one being the phasing of the work. With considerations of compound interest in mind, those responsible for the planning must decide whether to build the roads before planting begins or to defer the work until the first thinning is due. If the former course is adopted, there is an advantage in having a road for access during planting and subsequent operations, and also in the avoidance of later disturbance of the established plantation. But the interest on the outlay will accumulate over a longer period before the crop is felled and the money recouped.

If the building of the road is deferred, this period is reduced very considerably. There are also advantages in that more ground will have been available for planting and that the trees felled to make the road-trace will be saleable. The disadvantages lie in the considerable disturbance of the forest involved during the roading operations, which will tend to be more costly. Something of a compromise can be made by preparing the earthworks required before planting but deferring the expensive metalling until the first thinning is due. If this course is adopted, the use of the graded unmetalled surface must be strictly controlled to avoid the problems indicated above.

Season. The choice of the season for extraction will depend on a number of circumstances. Both summer and winter have their special advantages. In summer the ground conditions are likely to be better, that is to say drier, resulting in less damage to the soil structure through puddling or compaction. Summer extraction is also more acceptable to timber-merchants since it tends to be cleaner and easier, and therefore more economical; it also falls within the traditional non-felling period when their workmen are free to do the work. It has the disadvantages from the owner's point of view in that the land is sterilized for a season, with the result that immediate planting following felling is not possible; that the land is exposed for a whole summer to colonization by weed-seeds; that adjoining standing trees (or the whole of the remaining crop in the case of thinnings or group fellings) are more liable to damage while the sap is at full flow; and in woods where shooting is important, pheasants are disturbed during the nesting-season.

Winter extraction — or more correctly, winter-spring extraction — has the complementary advantages in that planting can be done immediately the ground is clear and relatively free of weeds; that the full sap-flow has not yet begun to run and the bark of standing trees is therefore less vulnerable to damage; and that a whole planting season is not lost. The corresponding disadvantages are that the winter conditions and the tight clearance schedule (made tighter on a shooting estate since the season ends on February 1st) are less attractive to timber merchants, and that the removal of lop-and-top is liable to be more difficult to achieve in time for planting. Experience has shown that insistence on the completion of clearance by the agreed date may, in a wet season, result in great damage to the site, and especially to the surface drainage.

Compaction of the soil. In clear-felled areas the weather, and therefore the state of the soil, at the time of timber extraction is crucial. The use of ever-heavier machines on increasingly-wider rubber tyres implies greater compaction of the soil. If this is already damp, the damage can be great, all the air being driven out of the upper layers and surface drainage completely destroyed.

It is often observed that clear-felling is followed by a strong growth of rushes. The commonly accepted explanation is that the removal of the trees results in the cessation of abstraction of water from the soil by their roots, and that there is in consequence an excess of water in the rooting layers. There may be some truth in this; but the concentration of rushes along discernible old extraction tracks suggests a very close correlation with soil-compaction, resulting in extreme cases in the puddling of wet clay.

Before these operations were mechanized, extraction of lighter loads was carried out by pole-waggons drawn by horses. The wheels of the waggons were iron-tyred. Under load they cut into the soil, but the tyres were narrow and the actual area compressed was very limited; and the ruts, though deep, closed easily and comparatively quickly. It is the writer's impression that heavy infestation by rushes in woodland areas where this type of vegetation was normally absent was not in those days a normal consequence of fellings in lowland broad-leaved woods, as it is today.

Damage to the bases of standing trees. Damage can be avoided when extracting timber in the length by providing buffers at critical points along the dragging-track. These may be in the form of standing trees of little value, deliberately left on an awkward corner, or even a clump of hazel. Although damage should be reduced wherever possible by these and other more conventional means, the examination of stumps of trees on a felled site has generally shown that little serious damage to the timber has actually been occasioned by the loss of fairly restricted areas of basal bark during extraction operations following periodical thinnings. This is found to be particularly the case with broad-leaved trees. In such cases a dark line can be seen in the butt with little or no development of rot. Nevertheless, it is advisable to give any such wounds as do occur the greatest possible opportunity of healing healthily by painting them. This will prevent the entry of wood-boring beetles before the callus-tissue has had time to heal over the wound.

Winching in the length. This method has advantages when a suitable tractor is available; but these are limited. It requires less work by the tractor along the racks and less saw-work in the close conditions of a young plantation. On the other hand, the dragging of logs or poles along the racks involves cutting up their surface, even when a skid-pan is used. The principal advantage lies in the convenience of being able to accumulate a large quantity of material at one site, outside the plantation, where cross-cutting and stacking of graded material can be carried out in optimum conditions. The principal disadvantage lies in the liability to damage to standing trees during the actual winching-out. Since to haul one piece at a time is obviously uneconomic it is usual to make a bunch of several pieces. The free ends of the pieces in such a bunch are apt to splay outwards and this can result in damage to trees standing along the side of the rack.

Cross-cutting at stump and extraction by buck-rake. There are several advantages in this method. An ordinary agricultural tractor can be used, as there is no need for a winch. The racks do not get cut up by dragging, and are in fact used to best advantage in that the tractor makes successive passes over a bed of small branchwood resulting from the trimming-out of the felled poles. The manual handling is limited to the sections that have been cross-cut and so are of reasonable size. By this system work proceeds in an orderly way, each load being made up of material of a similar grade and taken direct to the appropriate pile on the stacking ground.

Open drains and ditches. Drains and ditches are too often allowed to fill up with topwood and brush while clearance of felled timber is in progress; and if this is done on a wide scale the disturbance to the drainage of a site can be serious. Simple early planning can avoid this. Crossing-points for the ditches should be clearly marked in advance; there is no need to limit their numbers but their use must be observed strictly. At an early stage in felling, these crossing-points should be filled with strong topwood lengths to the level of their banks and slightly above, after first laying loops of steel-wire rope across the ditch. The wood will settle in deeply and firmly with the first few loads to cross; and when the extraction operation has been completed, the filling-material can be removed easily by a winch-tractor hauling on the wire-ropes. Provided that the work is done carefully, the main drainage system of the site can be preserved intact.

Is it worth doing? Where young broad-leaved crops are concerned, the question will often arise as to whether it is worth extracting the felled material after thinning. Occasions occur when considerable numbers of useful poles have been cut, of a size that could be sold, and there has been a strong feeling that they should be brought to account. No manager or owner of woodland likes to see produce lying in the wood that he knows could be sold. But the piecemeal extraction of small produce from a still dense crop of young trees is a laborious business that does not lend itself to mechanization. An example is provided by a case that occurred in the Cotswolds concerning small ash and sycamore poles cut during an early thinning of natural regeneration. It was only after a full-scale and carefully-costed trial that the owner came to accept that the cost of extracting the poles was too great for the operation to show a profit, even though there was a ready market for them. The irritating sight of saleable material left rotting at stump was dealt with by an instruction that only poles within ten metres of the wood-edge (that is, within sight from the rides) were to be extracted, this being a comparatively simple, easy, and cheap operation. The remaining poles were left lying in the wood.

It should always be borne in mind that the object of thinning a crop of trees is to provide adequate light and space to meet their expanding needs. If the material produced by the operation can be sold profitably, well and good; but a thinning operation that is silviculturally necessary should not have to justify itself financially. Early thinnings from conifer crops are often saleable; those from broad-leaved crops rarely find a market.

CHAPTER 23
Big Trees and Compound Interest

Britain is by nature a forest land like most other countries of Europe. When the ice-sheets of the last ice-age retreated northwards, trees rapidly colonized the bare land, and for several millennia the whole country was covered with forest growth. It was only with the gradual spread of man, with his fire and his flocks, that parts of the forest were converted into grassland and others into the blanket-peats of the uplands. This basic fact — that the forest was here before man — tends to be forgotten when considering forestry problems today. Yet it is highly relevant.

The Forestry Commission is the largest landowner in Great Britain, but the area it holds is actually considerably less than the total area of woodland in private hands. This latter fact is also apt to be forgotten by a public that is rightly impressed by the Commission's vast blanket plantings on the hillsides, while the older estate woodlands are accepted as a natural and proper part of the well-known country scene and excite little comment. With the Commission's activities dominating the forestry scene ever since its inception in 1919, it is perhaps inevitable that it should come to be regarded as synonymous with 'forestry', and its conceptions and methods the only ones to be adopted. And where bare ground is planted, this is not easily contested. Indeed, when the post-war phenomenon of investment planting developed to exploit the tax concessions then available to woodland owners, the methods adopted were those of the Commission. In the field of economics, the basic factor was the cost of establishing new plantations on bare ground.

That forests begin with bare ground is not axiomatic, as has been shown here. In the British tradition of land-ownership, in the past the opposite has normally been the case. An heir succeeding to a landed property inherited standing timber, not bare land to be planted. In fact, comparatively little planting of new land took place. Once an estate had been laid out it tended to retain its structure, planting normally being confined to the re-stocking which followed felling in the ordinary course of prudent estate management, in which amenity, game preservation, and timber production all had their part to play.

This somewhat parochial situation is comparable to the national situation of such traditional forest countries as France and Germany. Starting from a similar situation to Britain, where forest covered the whole land surface in post-glacial times, these countries have for the greater part of their history carried populations much lower than Britain in relation to their land area. Partly as a direct consequence of this, and partly no doubt as a result of their later start in industrial development, the proportion of these countries still under forest remains high when compared with Britain. With an ancient tradition of re-stocking their forests by means of natural regeneration, particularly in France, the concept of planting bare land has been far less dominant. The forest manager in European countries such as these starts, not with bare land, but with a forest.

It used to be said of the old French Service des Eaux et Forêts that it had a sufficiency of forest, a sufficiency of time, but no money. Until comparatively recently when political considerations have taken the security out of land ownership, similar conditions may be said to have applied to privately-owned estates in Britain. They had their existing woodland, time was not very relevant since the ownership passed down in the family from father to son, and few owners have ever in the recent past been prepared to spend much money on their woods.

Thus both nationally on the Continent of Europe and privately in Britain, the woods were there when the administrators or the individual owners assumed control over them. They were forests or woods, not bare land. When the time came to harvest the crop and re-stock the woods, there being no money available from other sources, this was found from the proceeds deriving from the felled trees. That is, the establishment of the new crop was reasonably regarded as a charge on the old one, the forest itself being a continuing organic entity. This is perhaps more clearly seen where silvicultural systems involving natural regeneration are employed. The work of seeding and final fellings, of opening strips or wedges, of cleaning in regeneration groups, and other silvicultural operations, are all part and parcel of the management of the forest. This integration is seen at its most perfect in the Selection System in which it is not possible to separate the cost of re-stocking from the cost of management of the forest as a whole. In all such systems the cost of the work involved is part of the continuing cost of managing the forest, and is paid for out of its continuing revenue.

If the matter is looked at historically, therefore, it will be seen that where re-stocking of felled woodland is concerned, as opposed to the afforestation of non-forestry land, the cost of replanting should in equity be a charge against the previous crop or, in wider terms, a part of the cost of maintaining a continuous forest. That being so, the costs involved should be deducted from the proceeds of the sale, which should be a net figure. The cost of re-stocking is thereby removed from the account.

The simple adoption of this totally different, but entirely logical, point of view could revolutionize forestry in this country. It would apply to almost all woods on traditional estates, and to all old woodland such as the New Forest and the Forest of Dean, in the hands of the Forestry Commission. It could be applied to all new plantings at the end of the first rotation.

It would remove much unreasonable stress from forestry. Too often, forestry is regarded either as an inefficient industrial process or as a form of agriculture. Rates of growth of trees are compared with the artificial interest rates generated by a highly-industrialized section of a commercially-orientated civilization. As a result of the application of compound interest in these conditions, forestry operations are shown to be 'uneconomic', and the use of long rotations for the production of high quality timber is ruled out. One result of this is that broad-leaved trees are regarded as an extravagance, only to be grown as a sop to an urban public which likes to see them.

It would be possible to abandon these attitudes and to grow trees with proper attention to their silvicultural requirements on rotations calculated to produce the highest quality product. There would no longer be the need to plant only the fastest-growing species, and all trees (including broad-leaves) could be grown to the optimum size to meet the demands of industry or amenity, or both.

It has long been obvious to many foresters that the criteria on which forestry has been judged were ill-chosen, and that the economic tools employed were often ill-devised. The Government's notorious Cost Benefit Analysis of some years ago stands as a supreme example of this. Calculations of financial rotations are meaningless when the value of money and rates of wages change from year to year; and net discounted revenue is no more than an arbitrary — even academic — means of comparing profitability in inflationary situations where rotations of up to 80 or even 120 years are being considered. The *reductio ad absurdum* is reached when the growing of oak on a rotation of 120 years is examined when interest rates were at 15 per cent. Assuming no interim yields, at compound interest a plantation costing £100 to plant would have to sell for £1,900,000,000 to break even on felling, without showing any profit.

The concept of a renewed crop costing nothing, and therefore carrying no burden of interest, would liberate British forestry from its present unhealthy and restricting straitjacket, and restore to it its ancient dignity as an essential, enduring, and in every way acceptable form of land use.

In the context of current attitudes towards forestry, by a public more concerned with conservation than with timber production, such a change would be revolutionary. Instead of the current short-rotation crops of fast-growing trees, the country could look forward to leaving to its successors the foundations of handsome forests such as visitors may admire in the old forests of the Continent of Europe, where beech, oak, spruce, and silver fir are still grown profitably to great size and beauty.

Index

Abies alba	10
Acer pseudoplatanus	7
Acidity	10
Access	1, 2
Acorns	8
Alder	29, 91
Alder, grey	75
Alnus glutinosa	29, 32, 91
Alnus incana	75
Amenity	1, 2, 35, 41, 46, 51
Annual rings	39, 40
Apple, crab	80
Apple, varieties	80
Ash	Ch. 2 8
	3 13, 14, 15, 21
	5 29, 30, 32
	9 56, 60
	11 69
	13 80, 82, 83
	14 91
	19 112, 113
	20 118
Ash, male	21
Ash, sports	115
Aspect	15
Aspen	32, 75

Aura	87
Avenues	65, 70
Axe-hafts	32
Bacterial canker	112
Bark	113, 114
Beansticks	30
Beech	Ch. 2 8, 9, 11, 15
	3 17, 18
	5 32
	6 38, 40, 41
	8 51
	9 60
	11 66, 69
	13 80
	14 88
	15 96
Beech sickness	14
'Belgian thinning'	118
Belgian turf planting	94, 95
Bellême, forest of	74
Belts	62, 69, 87
Betula spp.	8
Birch	Ch. 2 8
	3 21
	5 32
	6 38
	12 77
	17 104
	19 115, 116
Birds	4
Blanket-planting	87
Block	32
Bolton, Lord	125
Bradford, Lord	40
Bramble	100, 104
Branchwood	31
Brashing	103
Broadcast sowing	97
Broad-leaved woodland	34, 46
Brocklesby Estate	88
Brown, 'Capability'	2, 48, 70
Brown-earths	15
Brushwood	123, 127
Bud formation	9

Bulb-planter	20
Butt-length	41
Buttress	33
Calcicole	14
Callus-tissue	109
Canopy	10, 13, 17, 41
Carpenters	30
Carpinus betulus	32
Castanea sativa	29
Cedar, Atlas	11
Cedrus atlantica	11
Chalk	94
Chamaecyparis lawsoniana	40
Charcoal	30
Chemical build-up	99
Cherry, wild	14, 75, 76, 89, 108
Cheshire	103
Chestnut, sweet	29, 32, 75
Chilterns	14, 39, 40, 80, 112
Christchurch, Oxford	70
Christmas trees	44, 73
Clay	8
Clay-with-flints	15
Cleaning	103, 105
Clear-felling	2, 6, 10, 24, 44, 53
Climate	14, 87
Climatic climax	8
Climbers	38
Clumps	66, 68
Coal	30
Colbert	25
Colonizers	8
Compaction	14, 132
Compartments	61
Cones	10
Conifers	40, 46, 55, 89, 91, 115
Conservation	1, 3, 35, 41, 46
Conservation bodies	5
Continuous cover systems	1
Control of felling	61-64
Conversion to group selection	
of even-aged woods	47-52
of uneven-aged woods	53-60
Coppice	14, 19, 51, 75

143

Coppicing	91
Coppice-with-standards	29-36
Cording	58
Cornwall	32
Corridors	3
Corylus avellana	29
Cotswolds	8, 18, 19, 51, 56, 71, 80, 87
Cotyledons	17, 82
Coupes	30, 32, 44
Cross-colonization	6
Crown	42
Cruck houses	32
Cultivation by yew logs	18
Cycle	44
Dead trees, sale of	5
Deer	19, 41, 56
Denmark	18
De-wolfing	105
Devon	40
Dibbling	96, 97
Disease	4
'Domes' of regeneration	86
Douglas fir	40
Dragging-tracks	58
Drainage	15
'Drawn' trees	86
Dutch Elm Disease	70, 75
Earthworms	17
East Anglia	80
Ecosystems	3, 6, 46
Edge effect	85
Elm	32
Epicormic branching	34, 81
Erosion	40, 46
Even-aged woods	23
Exposure	40
Fagus sylvatica	8
Faggots	74
Farm forestry	53, 54
Fencing	32
Felling	125-128
Felling-cycle	47

Felling, direction of	126
Felling, final	26
Felling, timing of	125
Fir, silver	10
Firewood	30, 76, 91
Flint-gravel	15
Forest capital	35
Forestry Commission	25, 37, 62, 74, 79, 137
France	9, 10, 11, 13, 18, 19, 25, 26, 30, 38, 138
Fraxinus excelsior	8
Free growth	8, 41, 117
French Uniform System	10
Frost	9, 81, 83, 95, 101
Fuel	30, 31, 32
Garrigue	12
Genotypes	11
Geology	80
Germany	9, 30, 138
Germination	10, 17, 82
Gloucestershire	24, 118
Grafting, bud	21
Grants	3, 74
Grass	95
Grazing	7
Ground flora	13, 35
Groups	43
Groups, size of	86, 88
Group Selection System	1, 6, 43-46, 45, 19, 88, 126
Groves	66, 68
Growing stock	41
Hand-weeding	100
Hares	19
Harvesting	38, 44
Hazel	19, 29, 32, 87
Health	4
Heathers	30
Hedges	30, 31
Hedgerow trees	76
Herbicides	94
Herefordshire	14, 32
Hoeing	99
Hornbeam	32
Hurdle-stakes	30

Hygiene	4, 5
Ice-age	81
Increment	39
Inoculation	82
Insects	4, 9, 17
Insolation	48
Irregular woods	12
Irregular forestry	29
Jardinage	1, 2, 37
Jardinage par bouquets	2
Jays	8
Juglans regia	68
Jura, Swiss	100
Landes	10
Landscapers	2
Larch	19, 24, 32, 56, 57, 89
Larch, Japanese	115
Larix kaempferi	115
Lawson cypress	40, 96, 114
Leaders	81
Leaf-litter	14, 17, 82
Leaf-mould	12, 52
Ledbury	32
Light	3, 12, 13
Lime	32, 66, 75
Limestone	8, 11, 94
Lincolnshire	6, 47, 88
Line-transect	39
'Looking-glass planting'	66
Luberon	12
Maidens	33
Malaysia	9
Maple	32
Maritime pine	10
Marking for thinning	121, 122
Mast-years	9
Mechanical cleaning	19
Mice	8
Micro-climate	12, 14
Micro-flora	12
Micro-organisms	87

Migration of species	6
Mineral soils	17, 52, 97
Minerals	17
Mixtures	46, 87
Mulches	101
Mycorrhiza	82
Myxomatosis	11
Natural regeneration	7-15, 16, 23
New Forest	76
Nitrates	82
Normal forest	61, 62
Notch planting	95
Nursery	13, 21, 82
Nursing	89
Nutrients	13
Oak	*Ch.* 2 7, 10
	3 19
	5 29, 30, 31, 32
	9 56, 60
	11 66, 69
	14 89, 91
	15 96
	19 114
Oolite	19
Opening-up (canopy)	12
Outcrop	39
Ordnance Survey maps	72
Oxford Clay	8
Oxford University Department of Forestry	14
Pannage	17
Park planting	66, 67, 68
Park boundaries	70
Peasticks	30
Peat	30
Pebble-gravel	15
Pennines	80
Phenotypes	11
Pheasant-shooting	23, 30, 103
Photosynthesis	9
Picea abies	10
Pigeons	8, 17, 96
Pigs	18, 51

Pine, maritime	10
Pine, Scots	11, 26
Pinus pinaster	10
Pinus sylvestris	11
Pioneers	8, 12
Plane, oriental	68
Planting	79-98
Planting methods	94
Planting patterns	88, 90
Planting, pure	91
Planting systems	85-92
Platanus orientalis	68
Plastic mats	94, 95
Ploughing	94, 95
Podsols	15
Ponds	4
Poplar, white	75
Poplar, grey	75
Populus alba	75
Populus canescens	75
Populus tremula	32
Provenance	11, 21, 80
Pre-swiping	121
Prunus avium	14, 75
Pseudotsuga menziesii	40
Pulp	34, 91
Pyjama stripes	88
Pyrenees	11
Pyrus malus	80
Quality of plants	81
Quercus	7
Quercus robur	80
Rabbits	44, 56, 57, 76
Race	11, 80
Racks	129
Radiation	95
Regeneration planting	19
Region	80
Regular systems	23
Rendzina soils	14, 15
Repton, Humphrey	2, 48
Re-stocking	21, 73
Rides	3, 38

Ring width	114
Roads	3, 38, 130
Robinia	75
Robinia pseudoacacia	75
Root-hairs	82
Roots	13
Root-systems	81
Root-direction	94
Root-competition	111
Rotation	35, 44
Rotovators	18
Salix caprea	32
Sallow	32, 38, 104, 115
Sap flow	125
Scarifying	127
Scotland	32
Scots pine	26, 57, 69, 79
Screens	46, 69
Screefing	94, 101
Scrub	56
Seaweed solution	94
Second-rotation crops	73
Seed	7, 10
Seed-bearers	11
Seed-dispersal	10
Seed dormancy	13
Seeding-felling	10, 26
Selection System	1, 10, 37-42, 38, 100, 115, 139
'Selective felling'	14, 40
Services des Eaux et Forêts	25
Shade-bearing	8, 41
Shading	4, 10, 113
Shake	81
Sheep	76, 77
Shelter	6, 48
Shelters, plastic	21, 96
Shelter-belts	71
Shelterwood	13
Shooting stands	29, 51
Silver fir	38, 40
Silviculture	9
Site conditions	8
Skyline	71
Sleeves, protective	19

Small woods	53
Snow	40
Soils	10
Soils, acid	19
Soils, arable	94
Soils, calcareous	19
Sorbus aria	14
Sowing, direct	96
Space	10
Space sharing	39
Spekewood	30
Sport	2, 3, 105
Spraying, spot	95
'Springs'	31
Spruce	38
Squirrels	8, 17, 41, 56, 76
Stability	87
Standards	29
Stick thinning	120
Stimulation	86
Stool	30, 32, 33
Storm-damage	13
Stumps	126
Suckers	75
Sugar	9
Sunspot-cycle	9
Surrey	32
Sustained yield	25, 48
Swine	17
Swipe	105
Switzerland	9, 38, 62
Sycamore	*Ch.* 2 7, 14
	3 21
	5 29
	9 56, 60
	13 80, 82
	14 91
	20 118
Tap-root	96
Tarmac	11
Tavistock	40
Taxation of woodland	139
Taxus baccata	15
Teller	33

151

Thatching spars	30
Thinning	26, 111-124
Thinning, by oblique cut	124
Thinning, by poisoning	123
Thinning cycle	88
Thuja plicata	40
Tilia spp.	32
Timber	30, 32, 33, 41, 48, 80
Timber Growers Organization	109
Tolerant species	38
Topping of big trees	128
Transplanting	20, 81
Tronçais, forêt de	74
Tropics	7
Tsuga heterophylla	59
Turf planting	94
Turnery	76
Ulmus glabra	56
Ulmus spp.	32
Under-cutting	81
Underwood	31
Uniform System	10, 13, 19, 26, 27
Valuation	6
Variant	80
Variety	80
Vaucluse	11
Vermin	76
Virgin forest	7
Vistas	46
Visual amenity	51
Voles	8
Volume	39
Volunteer growth	13
Wales, South	80
Walnut	68
Water	17
Wattle-and-daub	30
Wedge-felling	48, 49, 50, 52, 69
Wedge System, German	48, 51
Weed-trees	115
Weeding	99-102
Weeding, mechanized	93

Weeding, spraying	93
Weeds	10
Western hemlock	59
Western red cedar	40, 89, 96, 114
Wheelwright	30
Whips	112
Whitebeam	14
Wilderness	2
Wildlife	3, 35
Willow	32
Wind	40, 44, 49
Windsor estate	26
Wind-rowing brush	123
Withybed	31
Wolf-trees	105
Woodrush	15
Wurttemburg Black Forest	48
Wych elm	56
Yew	15, 18, 32
Yield	41
Yield control	62
Yield tables	63
Yorkshire	69, 80, 82, 83